# Build Your Own Rainbow

## *A Workbook for Career and Life Management*

# Build Your Own Rainbow

## A Workbook for Career and Life Management

by
## Dr. Barrie Hopson
and Mike Scally

**Pfeiffer**
**& COMPANY**

Johannesburg • London
San Diego • Sydney • Toronto

*Published in Association With*

**Published by Pfeiffer & Company**
8517 Production Avenue
San Diego, California 92121
United States of America
Editorial Offices:
(619) 578-5900, FAX (619) 578-2042
Orders:
(U.S.A.) (606) 647-3030, FAX (606) 647-3034

Originally published in the UK by Mercury Books.

**Library of Congress Catalog-in-Publication Data**

Hopson, Barrie.
  Build your own rainbow: a workbook for career and life management /
by Barrie Hopson and Mike Scally.
      p.  cm.
  "Published in association with Lifeskills Learning."
  Includes index.
  ISBN 0-89384-208-7 (trade pbk.) : ISBN 0-88390-381-4 (professional pbk.)
  1. Success—Psychological apects.  2. Self-actualization (Psychology)
  I. Scally, Mike,  II. Title.
BF637.S8H614    1993
158'.1—dc20                                                          92-50992
                   Printed in the United States of America.            CIP
              Printing        4 5 6 7 8 9 10

# Contents

# Acknowledgments

This book represents 20 years of work and development. It took only months to write but those 20 years are written into every page. We have found that the rationale and the techniques it contains have been of immense value to us personally and that experience has been echoed by the thousands of people who have also experienced the career and life management programs that form the basis of the book.

There are many special acknowledgments we wish to make:

- Florence Lewis of Bank America, California
- Jack Loughary of the University of Oregon
- Dick Knowdell of Career Testing and Design, San Jose
- Donald Super of Teachers College, Columbia University for ideas, suggestions, and feedback
- Hobson's Press for permission to reproduce the self-employment questionnaire from "Your Own Business"
- Everyone who has participated and contributed to all of those workshops over 20 years and who thereby have helped us to build our rainbow
- The more than 150 development testers of the Open University in the U.K. who piloted the materials

This book is significant for us both in another, very relevant way. Both our careers have been characterized by a cyclical career pattern. When we wrote the first edition of this book in the U.K. in 1984, we had just resigned from our full-time posts as Director and Deputy Director of the Counseling and Career Development Unit at Leeds University to form Lifeskills Associates. We had spent eight marvelous years building that particular rainbow.

In 1989 we split Lifeskills Associates into two companies: Lifeskills Communications and Hay-Lifeskills, a joint venture with the Hay Group. Predictably for us, this year is another major change for us as we leave Hay-Lifeskills in the U.K. in other capable hands and have formed the Lifeskills Group of companies with Peter Gannon, the managing director of Lifeskills Communications. As you see, rainbows do not last forever, even ones that you build for yourself. As one begins to fade, another is waiting to be built. The Lifeskills Group is our current rainbow—until the next one...

Be a Rainbow Builder—you can manage your life and your career. This book is an invitation to begin now.


Barrie Hopson and Mike Scally

Yorkshire, England,

March 1993

# Introduction

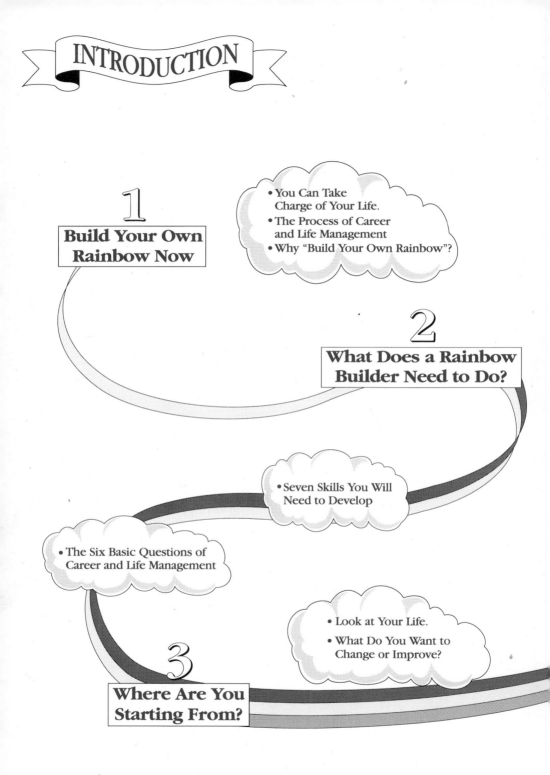

INTRODUCTION

1 Build Your Own Rainbow Now

• You Can Take Charge of Your Life.
• The Process of Career and Life Management
• Why "Build Your Own Rainbow"?

2 What Does a Rainbow Builder Need to Do?

• Seven Skills You Will Need to Develop

• The Six Basic Questions of Career and Life Management

3 Where Are You Starting From?

• Look at Your Life.
• What Do You Want to Change or Improve?

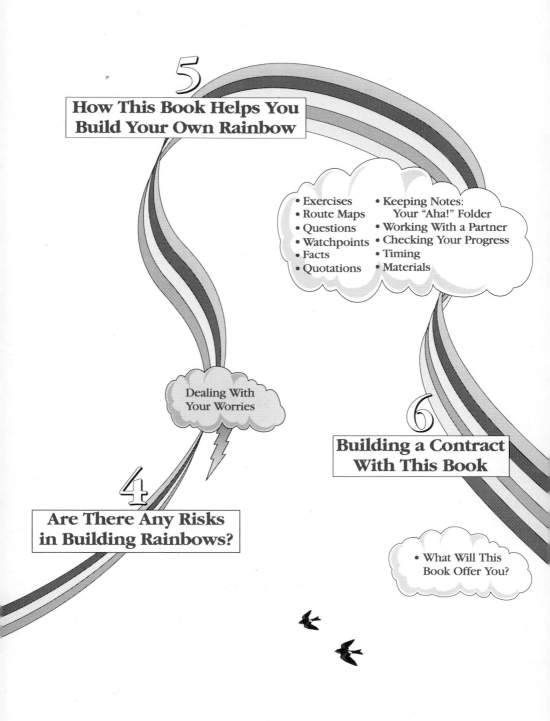

**5**

**How This Book Helps You Build Your Own Rainbow**

• Exercises
• Route Maps
• Questions
• Watchpoints
• Facts
• Quotations

• Keeping Notes:
  Your "Aha!" Folder
• Working With a Partner
• Checking Your Progress
• Timing
• Materials

Dealing With
Your Worries

**6**

**Building a Contract With This Book**

**4**

**Are There Any Risks in Building Rainbows?**

• What Will This
  Book Offer You?

# Build Your Own Rainbow Now!

Here is Edward Bear, coming downstairs now, bump, bump, on the back of his head behind Christopher Robin. It is, as far as he knows, the only way of coming downstairs, but sometimes he feels there really is another way, if only he could stop bumping for a moment and think of it.

A.A. Milne, *Winnie the Pooh*

## You Can Take Charge of Your Life

Edward Bear's experience is, unfortunately, not totally unfamiliar to most of us at times. You may be aware of a vague dissatisfaction or perhaps even a major problem. You worry, feel anxious, or do not seem to be getting anywhere. Indeed, you are not sure of your destination or even how to recognize that you have arrived. That is exactly the time to "stop your world and get off"; to examine your life from the outside and yourself from the inside.

There is a game people often play called:
It will be different when…

- I've passed my exams.
- I've left school.
- I've gotten my promotion.
- I've changed jobs.
- I'm married.
- We have children.
- The children leave home.
- I retire.

If you are not careful, the months, and then the years can go by as you wait and yet never really take charge of your life. The habit of waiting for things to happen can develop early in life. Hence, early in life you need to begin to believe and to demonstrate that

- There is always an alternative.
- Tomorrow need not be like today.
- Things do not have to be going badly before they can get better.

5

Each of us has 168 hours to live each week. For a 30-year-old with an average life expectancy of 75 years, that equals a total of 393,120 hours left to live. With such a huge investment of time—an ever-decreasing resource, it is not unreasonable to ask

- What return am I getting on the way I am currently spending my time?
- What return do I want?
- At the end of my life, what will I need to have done to be able to say I made the best use of my time?

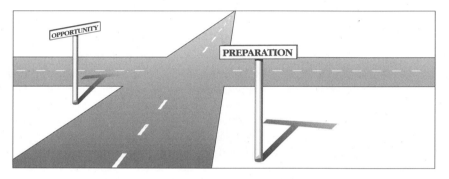

*Luck is the crossroads where preparation and opportunity meet.*

## The Process of Career and Life Management

Clearly, accidents in life happen to everyone. There will always be factors over which you have little or no control, but many people ascribe to fate the good or bad things that happen to them and minimize their own contributions to events.

### *Pinball-living or Self-empowerment?*

Dissatisfactions flow from what we call "pinball-living." Balls in a pinball machine have no life of their own; they are set in motion by someone else and then bounce from one place to another without any clear direction.

The opposite to pinball living is self-empowered living. Self-empowerment is a process by which you increasingly take greater charge of yourself and your life. To operate in a self-empowered way entails being able to

- Believe and operate in the belief that you are open to and able to change.
- Have the skills to change some aspects of yourself and the world in which you live.
- Use your feelings to recognize where there is a discrepancy between the way things are and the way you would like them to be.
- Specify desired outcomes and the necessary action steps.
- Act—to implement your action plans.
- Live each day being aware of your power to assess, review, influence, and self-direct.
- Help others to become more self-empowered.

To become more self-empowered you need to know the answers to the following questions:

- What is important to me in life?
- What do I want to do with my life?
- What beliefs will help me to get what I want?
- What information do I need about myself and our world?
- What skills do I need to get me what I want?

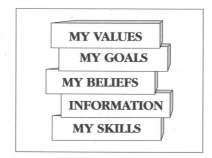

*The building blocks for personal change.*

## Why "Build Your Own Rainbow"?

Throughout history a rainbow has been a symbol of hope and achievement. In China it is viewed as the bridge between this world and paradise. In India it represents the highest attainable yogic state. In our every day Western world it is often viewed as ephemeral and beautiful—beautiful perhaps because of its ephemerality.

What do you think of when you think about rainbows?

Sit back, close your eyes. Picture a rainbow. What do you see? What feelings does it trigger for you?

We have chosen to build this book around a rainbow because to many people it represents hope, beauty, and optimism. Career and life management is a process that can enable you to make your life more like you want it to be. You do not have to wait for the chance meeting of rain and sun to provide a rainbow. You can build your own rainbow. It is within your grasp.

Another part of rainbow mythology is the famed pot of gold that can be found at the spot where the rainbow touches the earth. People who try to find the elusive pot of gold by chasing rainbows are often called daydreamers or viewed as idealists with their heads in the clouds due to their habit of hoping for impossible things. And we would agree—to a point. There is little to gain from hoping for impossible things, but planning is the best way we know of converting the impossible into the realm of the possible.

Perhaps the "rainbow chasers" make their mistakes in assuming that the pots of gold are "out there" somewhere, waiting to be found. True "rainbow builders" know that the treasure lies within themselves waiting to be molded and formed into images constrained mainly by the limits of their own imaginations.

The rainbow is the *vision.*

The tools we need to build our rainbows are our *skills.*

The clouds on the horizon are *questions* we need
to answer before we can build our rainbows.

# What Does a Rainbow Builder Need to Do?

## The Six Basic Questions of Career and Life Management

### 1. *Who Am I?*

- What are my transferable skills, my values, my interests?
- How do I spend my time?
- Where do I want to live and work?

### 2. *Where Am I Now?*

- Which stage of life am I at?
- What kind of career pattern do I want?

### 3. *How Satisfied Am I?*

This will involve an analysis of all your important life roles: child, student, employee, friend, consumer, citizen, pleasure seeker, homemaker, and, if appropriate, spouse and parent.

### 4. *What Changes Do I Want?*

A perfectly legitimate answer can be "none." This does not render the earlier questions useless. In reviewing your life you may discover that you really like much of what it contains. Reviewing your life can provide new or renewed commitment to aspects of present living. You may discover that you need to make some minor changes but that the major elements of your life are fulfilling.

On the other hand, you may reach some very dramatic decisions—to change jobs, shift careers, get married or divorced, start a family, take up new interests, relinquish old ones. You may discover that goals that you set years ago are no longer appropriate.

Your own personal goals and needs may have stayed constant, but social changes can result in your being stuck with them, with the mainstream of social and technological development leaving you further behind.

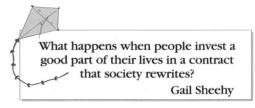

What happens when people invest a good part of their lives in a contract that society rewrites?
Gail Sheehy

You may need to review not only your goals and behavior, but also fundamental beliefs that label you as a product of a former age.

Let your imagination soar. There is a time for keeping one's feet on the ground, but that only comes after you have soared to the limits of your imagination. In rainbow building you are encouraged to daydream, to fantasize, to explore ideals, to free yourself from the shackles of everyday life and its commitments.

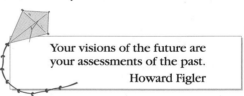

Your visions of the future are your assessments of the past.
Howard Figler

## 5. *How Do I Make Changes Happen?*

Deciding what to change is the first vital step toward change. We all know that the road to hell is paved with good intentions. It is rarely paved with good objectives, because a good objective will lead you toward what you want to happen. The next step is to construct an action plan capable of achieving that objective. The final step is simply "to do it." That last step sounds the simplest but is sometimes the most difficult. It will become easier the better we become at objective setting and action planning. We may also need the help and support of other people to do this.

## 6. *What If My Plan Doesn't Work Out?*

However thorough your self-analysis, however brilliant your vision, however systematic your objectives and action plans, there is no guarantee that you can always build your rainbow as you want or when you want. How do you cope with the frustration and disappointment?

This is where "Look After Yourself" skills are particularly crucial. A failed objective is simply that—a failed objective. It doesn't make you a failure. It simply means that your objective was unrealistic or not sufficiently well thought out. Failures need to be viewed more like undesirable computer feedback on a space flight. It may be necessary to adjust course, or even abort the mission, but the promise of success will always have justified the attempt and much will have been learned for future missions.

> Generally it is our failures that civilize us.
> Triumph confirms us in our habits.
> Clive James

## Seven Skills You Will Need to Develop

Set Objectives and Make Action Plans
Learn From Experience
Know Yourself
Research Skills
Make Decisions
Look After Yourself
Communicate

A rainbow builder needs to have access to all seven skills illustrated above. This book will enable you to develop all of these skills. You will need to *Look After Yourself* throughout the process. You will frequently need to *Communicate* with others, reassess your values and skills (*Know Yourself*), review what has happened (*Learn From Experience*), *Set Objectives* and *Make Action Plans*, and consequently will need to find out more information (*Research Skills*) as a result of which you will need to *Make Decisions*.

We are offering you a process, based on the six career and life management questions. If you follow it, it will help you to find your own answers to what you want to do with your career and your life. Let's examine the seven skills in more detail.

## 1. *Know Yourself*

To be a rainbow builder you need to have a thorough understanding of your raw materials, which in this case means *you*. The analogy with building is not strictly accurate. Once objects are built their structure and appearance stay primarily the same. You, however, are subject to change, indeed, the very process of introspection and analysis will influence the person you are and will become.

For effective career and life management to take place, you need to know how to get information on

- *Values:* What is important to you in life?
- *Transferable Skills:* What can you do and what do you enjoy doing?
- *Interests:* What activities are of interest to you irrespective of your skill levels?

You live within the context of the life that you have built and that has developed around you. Thus, you also need to know how to get information on your present style of living.

- How you presently spend your time: What do you do? With whom? How often? For how long?
- Where you live.
- Current Life Stage: Do you know what life stages there are and where you are in relation to them?
- Career Pattern Desired: Do you want one or a number of occupations? How many hours do you want to spend in paid work? How much variety do you need?

## 2. *Learn From Experience*

Some people never seem to learn from experience. They frequently seem to repeat mistakes. Why is that? It might stem from a failure to analyze an experience to see what can be learned from it. We call this process reviewing. It involves being able to

- Describe an experience.
- Identify what has been learned from it.
- Generalize that learning to other situations.

## 3. *Research Skills*

To obtain self-knowledge you need to develop the skills of looking inward, but the skills of accessing information outside of yourself are what we call research skills. You will need to know how to get information from

- Key people in your life in terms of how they think you are doing.
- Other people, printed materials, and community resources.

## 4. *Set Objectives and Make Action Plans*

A popular poster states: "If you don't know where you're going, you'll probably end up somewhere else." Many people fail to get what they want in life because they have never figured out exactly what they do want. They experience dissatisfaction, they know something isn't right but they have never really developed the skills of converting complaints into aims, aims into objectives, and objectives into action plans.

An *aim* is a general statement of what one wants to happen—"I want a job."

An *objective* is an aim made more specific—"I want to get a job as a car mechanic."

An *action plan* describes the steps that have to be completed before bringing that about.

Often prior to setting objectives you may need to let your imagination soar to explore a wide range of possibilities. Then you need to narrow down the possibilities. The figure shows how this process occurs: always broaden the horizons and then narrow them down.

| **STEP 1**<br>Identify<br>Possibilities | Supermarket Manager<br>Computer Programmer<br>Work with children<br>Electrician<br>Plumber<br>Work outdoors<br>Car Mechanic<br>Work with people<br>Engineer | Electrician<br>Car Mechanic<br>Work with people | **STEP 2**<br>Narrow<br>Down |

Some people do not find it easy to let their imaginations soar and need help to learn to do so. Objective and action planning skills, therefore, involve knowing how to

- Convert your complaints into achievable objectives.
- Fantasize freely.
- Discover the parts of your life you wish to change.
- Set objectives.
- Make action plans.

## 5. *Make Decisions*

The more information you collect about yourself and the world around you, the easier it is to become paralyzed by it. The ability to generate alternative choices based upon the information and having strategies for deciding between them is crucial.

## 6. *Look After Yourself*

No one said that building rainbows is easy. Career and life management can be a demanding process. Finding out about oneself can be very intellectually and emotionally trying. You can unearth aspects that make you feel uncomfortable. You may be forced to face up to challenging questions about how you are currently living your life. At the end of the process, with your rainbows carefully planned out, you might not be able to achieve your objectives. A vital skill, therefore, is to be able to look after oneself physically, mentally, and emotionally during the process, especially when things do not turn out as planned. This involves being skilled in stress management and stress prevention.

## 7. *Communicate*

Career and life management will always involve a considerable degree of self-determination; however, the effective use of other people is also crucial to the process. You need feedback from others. You have to ask for help and information. You need to be able to express yourself clearly both verbally and in writing.

# Where Are You Starting From?

Your rainbow can be approached from one of many starting points. This book offers a pathway to finding and building your rainbow. All of the starting points begin from a sense that something could be different or better in your life. This can range in intensity from a feeling of major crisis to an interest in checking out whether you are getting as much as you could out of life. The following clouds all represent reasons for using this book.

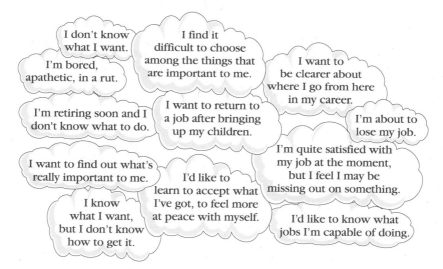

I don't know what I want.

I find it difficult to choose among the things that are important to me.

I'm bored, apathetic, in a rut.

I want to be clearer about where I go from here in my career.

I'm retiring soon and I don't know what to do.

I want to return to a job after bringing up my children.

I'm about to lose my job.

I want to find out what's really important to me.

I'm quite satisfied with my job at the moment, but I feel I may be missing out on something.

I'd like to learn to accept what I've got, to feel more at peace with myself.

I know what I want, but I don't know how to get it.

I'd like to know what jobs I'm capable of doing.

List any others that might be true for you.

In the clouds below, write your three most important reasons for using this book. At the end of this book you will review these to see whether or not you have learned any skills for building your rainbows.

## Look at Your Life

Lives, however hard we might try, cannot be completely compartmentalized. A job change is bound to affect other areas of your life. Changing a leisure habit may have consequences for how you spend your spare time and may have an impact on your family life. This book is designed to enable you to review your life as you are living it now, in total. Let us examine some of the parts that together make up the whole that is your life.

The hardest battle is to be nobody but yourself in a world, which is doing its best, night and day, to make you everybody else.

e.e. cummings

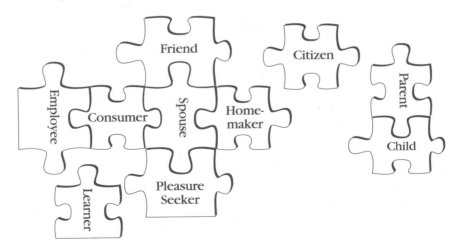

In the course of your lifetime you will occupy a variety of the roles illustrated by the jigsaw pieces. Sometimes they will connect with one another, sometimes they will not, and some will be in conflict periodically. How you live out your life roles will be influenced by a number of other key concepts that we will examine briefly.

## What Do You Want to Change or Improve?

### *Work*

By this we do not mean simply "paid employment." Work refers to activities that can provide you with a

- Sense of purpose and direction.
- Structure for living, be it regular or irregular.
- Personal sense of identity and self-respect.
- Source for companions and friends.
- View of how others see and feel about you.

In addition, work can provide money if someone wants to pay for what you can do. Work does not automatically provide you with money. Only paid work does that, which is why we distinguish work from jobs (see "Your Work Values"). You work in the process of planning and implementing any of your life roles. You may be paid for some of that work.

### *Job*

This is a particular position of employment one holds at any one time.

### *Play*

This refers to pleasurable activities enjoyed just for their own sake.

### *Income*

Monies received from paid work, investments, or other sources.

### *Career*

This is the pattern of jobs that you have had, have now, or hope to have. Everyone has a "career" in this sense, even when it has periods of unemployment, involves retraining or learning, or varies from forty hours a week to one hour a week.

## *Leisure*

The time at your discretion after any paid work or day-to-day maintenance activities have been done is leisure time. It can include both
unpaid work and play.

# Are There Any Risks in Building Rainbows?

I will get dissatisfied. If I stay as I am then I will be all right.

I might want to make dramatic changes and that could create
problems for others.

No one should be *made* to review their lives. Rainbows cannot be
forced! However, most people benefit from occasional reviews. The
parallel is visiting your family doctor. Do you consult a doctor only
when ill? You would be better advised to have periodic check-ups,
and, as a consequence, you might get ill less often.

There is no doubt that
confronting your dissatisfactions can be a very unset-
tling and sometimes painful
experience. As with your
body, however, you can
only feel pain if something

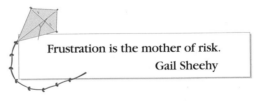

Frustration is the mother of risk.
                                    Gail Sheehy

is wrong and needs attention. Pain is often a prerequisite to healing
and growth.

Sometimes you will have to experience frustration before you can
be motivated to want to change.

You may be happy with things as they are, but your situation may
change dramatically and create a problem as a result. Social and technological developments may not allow you to stand still. Remember
that you usually need storms to bring rainbows!

## Dealing With Your Worries

All too often people use the anticipated fears and objections of others to mask their own anxieties and concerns. How many times have you heard or made statements like "I could never do that, my spouse/family would never go along with it"? Check and see if it is a real concern.

The following story illustrates the dangers of being nonassertive about one's own needs and not checking things out with others.

> One (and we are not saying which one!) of our in-laws arrived to spend the weekend. My wife and I were not quite sure what to do with them, yet we felt that we should make an effort to do something. We normally looked to our weekends for recuperation, and our idea of a good time is to do nothing—lie in bed and get up naturally, do exactly what we feel like doing, stay at home and enjoy being at home—a luxury for us. However, though neither of us wanted to do anything, we thought we should offer to take them out—at least on Sunday. We asked them if they wished to tour the Yorkshire Dales. They said they would, so we all set off.
>
> I was doing my best to be cheery, wishing all the time that I was at home reading the Sunday papers. My wife was doing her best trying to keep me happy and to give her parents a good time, consequently succeeding only in giving herself a headache. We took them to a favorite pub for lunch—which didn't do lunch on Sundays! We drove them around the Dales in a force-eight gale punctuated by occasional thunderstorms. The final straw was a flat tire that I had to repair in the rain. Six hours later when we got home, I could contain myself no longer. "Well, I think in the future we'll stick to our usual Sunday routine."
>
> "What's that?" they asked. So I told them. "That sounds wonderful. We're exhausted after the week we've had. We would have loved a quiet time with our feet up."
>
> "Why didn't you say anything?" I said through tight lips.
>
> "You both seemed so determined to go out, we didn't like to disappoint you. We thought that this was probably how you both liked to spend your Sundays."

Do you often make assumptions about the needs of others and remain nonassertive about your own? What if your desires really do clash with those of people close to you? Our answer to that would be that probably all this process has done has brought forward in time something that would have happened in any case. Where differences exist, it is usually better to bring them out into the open where they can be examined, negotiated if necessary, or at least given an open discussion about the differences.

"What does it say about me if I keep changing my mind about what I want?" It says simply that you are normal. You are more rather than less likely to change with the years. Between young adulthood and middle-age (a twenty-year period) people have been shown to change fifty-two percent of their interests, fifty-five percent of their vocational interests, sixty-nine percent of their self-rated personality characteristics, and ninety-two percent of their answers to questions about their attitudes. The research that demonstrated this was carried out by E.L. Kelly in 1955. What would the equivalent research show today with the more dramatic rate of social change?

Often you decide on goals for yourself in your teens or twenties, then age and develop, yet still work toward goals that may not be appropriate to the different person that you have become.

> "All my life, or at least it seemed that way, I had wanted to be the director of _____. It is only now that I realize that the real reason I wanted that in my twenties was that then I couldn't think of any other criteria of real success. It's taken me until now to realize that I have been successful in so many ways—in my work, with the family life I have created, in my circle of friends. And you know, if I really look at the way the director lives, I wouldn't want that lifestyle. Yet, I've struggled for years to get somewhere I now know I don't want to get to and I've been giving myself a bad time for not getting there."
>
> A Marketing Manager of a large company, aged 46

We were very impressed with some advertising copy selling a particular make of car and thought it was very relevant to career and life management: "Having arrived doesn't mean much if you're bored getting there."

> I can have all the "fantasies" I like, but I am still limited by what's available and what I will be allowed to do.

There is no denying that there are very real constraints operating on you no matter how self-empowered you are. You cannot single-handedly change the economy, prevent political disaster, give yourself talents that you do not possess, or turn back your biological clock. But people consistently overestimate the factors over

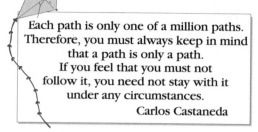

Each path is only one of a million paths. Therefore, you must always keep in mind that a path is only a path. If you feel that you must not follow it, you need not stay with it under any circumstances.

Carlos Castaneda

which they can have no influence and underestimate those that they can influence.

One of our favorite posters says: "You can either have what you want or have the excuse for not having it." That, as a statement of fact, is somewhat dubious—but it makes the point.

Rainbows begin in the clouds and that is where you need to begin also. Life's constraints are all too obvious and can prevent you from exercising your imagination. The view from the clouds can be very different from the limited horizons you can see from the ground. Having seen it, we may choose to return to earth in a different place.

Similarly, there is often a distinction between what you can do and what you think society says that you should do. Sometimes you fail to begin to build rainbows because you are the "wrong" age, the "wrong" sex, or because you lack "qualifications." Age stereotyping is very real and happens all the time. You can explore your own attitudes to aging and discover how far you yourself contribute to "ageism" (see Exercise 13). Much age stereotyping is reflected in social attitudes and is rarely based on facts.

Expectations based on gender undoubtedly are a very real barrier to rainbow building. Legislation has helped to widen horizons for both sexes, but the current research findings are depressingly predictable. Teachers encourage boys more in their learning and career aspirations; parents still behave differently to the sexes, even before birth. Employers are still blinded by the assumptions of yesteryear. We all have a vital role in working for a future in which there are not two sets of rainbows, but one in which all people can share.

I don't like the idea of planning for the future. It takes away all the spontaneity from life.

Career and life management is not dedicated to forcing people to plan their lives away. It is dedicated to helping people gain more control over what happens to them. Our personal preference is to plan no more than six to twelve months ahead. Other people like to create five-year, ten-year, or lifelong plans. There is no right or wrong way. Those of us with short-term inclinations could do well to force ourselves occasionally to look long term, and lifelong planners need to remind themselves that any long-term plan needs a periodic review.

The seeming paradox of career and life management is that the more attention you give to reviewing your needs, to determining your priorities, and to setting objectives, the more likely you are to provide yourself with gift vouchers of time to exchange for anything you, spontaneously, might choose to do.

> What happens if I try to make changes and I don't get what I
> want? Am I worse off than before I started?

We believe that the straight answer has to be "No." Unless we risk change, we will never gain access to its fruits. Rainbow building will rarely leave you worse off even if it doesn't turn out as desired. The process of career and life management will involve you in learning a

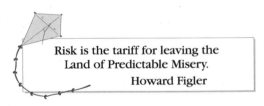

Risk is the tariff for leaving the
Land of Predictable Misery.
Howard Figler

great deal about yourself and also in developing the seven crucial rainbow-building skills that you can use on other occasions.

Perhaps the final rejoinder will always remain: "If you don't try it, you'll never know just what you can build for yourself."

Each of us will have opportunities sometimes. The better equipped you are with career and life management skills, the greater the chance of being able to capitalize on those opportunities. Carlos Castenada talks of the importance of recognizing our "cubic centimeters of chance"—the skill of recognizing chances when they occur and having the courage to pursue them.

> All of us, whether or not we are warriors, have a cubic centime-
> ter of chance that pops up in front of our eyes from time to
> time. The difference between the average man and the warrior
> is that the warrior is aware of this, and one of his tasks is to be

alert and deliberately waiting so that when his cubic centimeter pops up he has the speed, the prowess to pick it up.

Carlos Castaneda

Remember, it is only if you want to be mediocre that you don't have to try to be your best!

# How This Book Helps You Build Your Own Rainbow

## Exercises

The book contains exercises designed to help you collect data to answer the six key questions for career and life management. Some space is provided for writing in your answers. These exercises are there to help you and should not represent an obstacle course. If any particular exercise does not seem relevant to you, don't do it.

Each exercise is also designed to help you develop one of the seven key career and life management skills. The particular skill or skills will be indicated at the beginning of an exercise. The asterisked* exercises are the ones that we believe to be crucial to building your own rainbows. We have included additional exercises that could be illuminating; if time is short, you might skip these or leave them until later.

You may choose not to complete some of the optional exercises because they are not relevant to you or where you are now. Beware, however, that you may not feel like completing some of them because of what they will reveal to you. If this is the case, ask yourself if that is sufficient reason for not doing the exercise.

## Route Maps

Each of the six career and life management questions will be introduced by a Route Map that will be your guide to where answering the question will take you. The map will outline the exercises contained along the route.

Periodically in the text you will see a picture of a notebook. This will tell you when you need to make notes and keep a record.

You might wish to keep your answers in an actual file card box, but failing this, keep them in your "Aha!" folder (see "Keeping Notes: Your 'Aha!' Folder").

Occasionally, you will see a card like this:

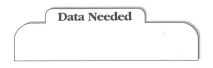

This always refers you back to "keep a record" files from earlier exercises. Your journey to building your own rainbow is not a simple straight line. There will be considerable cross-referencing.

You will sometimes be referred forward in the book. This will always be to some part of Question 6: "What If It Doesn't Work Out?" Throughout the book you will be invited to explore yourself, your past, your vision, your fears, your assumptions. Some of this can be very demanding and even painful. The information in Question 6 could be very useful long before you would reach it in the book.

Here are some other features of the text for you to be aware of:

## Questions

The book constantly offers you questions to further your self-discovery process. These are always heralded by a cloud and question mark.

## Watchpoints

This symbol tells you how to interpret something in the text. Watch for these! They are important.

## Facts

We think it crucial to make decisions from an informed position. Throughout the book we provide what we believe to be particularly important information and statistics to stimulate your thinking. Each piece of data is heralded by this heading.

## Quotations

We fly a number of quotations throughout the book in kites. These are intended to stimulate, summarize, or amuse. Some will speak to you more than others.

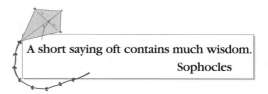

A short saying oft contains much wisdom.
Sophocles

## Keeping Notes: Your "Aha!" Folder

In doing this kind of self-review, many insights or "Aha!" experiences can result from completing the exercises, particularly in discussing them with a partner or group. We advise keeping a separate folder in which you put slips or sheets of paper with any insights that occur to you about yourself, your life, or your career. Toward the end of the workbook we will ask you to empty the contents of your "Aha!" folder and use them as an aid to setting your objectives. Remember, there are no right answers, only answers that are right for you.

## Working With a Partner

A particularly valuable strategy when faced with hours of isolated work is to link up with another person or a small group of people. We highly recommend this. Talking through these exercises will not only assist flagging motivation but also you will find that other people's reactions to your efforts and thoughts are likely to be valuable and stimulating (in turn, your reactions to their ideas could be useful, too).

A phrase we often quote is: "It takes two to see one." It can sometimes be enlightening to involve family, friends, and colleagues in completing some of the assignments. It can also be scary! We do not recommend choosing someone who could feel threatened by what you are doing or who might put you down or otherwise inhibit you. Perhaps you could link up with some fellow "rainbow builders" who also contract to work with the book themselves. A clear contract is essential. It should cover the following points:

- When are you going to meet?
- How often and for how long?
- What work will you have to complete for each session?
- How will you operate as a pair or a group?

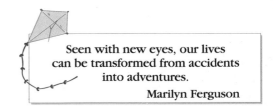

Seen with new eyes, our lives can be transformed from accidents into adventures.

Marilyn Ferguson

## Checking Your Progress

Throughout the book there will be opportunities to pause, review your progress, and preview what is to come. At the end of each of the six cloud questions, there is a summary chart to help you to consolidate all of your data for that question.

## Timing

We have deliberately not suggested times for the exercises. We have found that people need to spend different amounts of time for the same exercises. We do suggest that you ensure that you have sufficient time to finish a "block" on your route map. The end of a block is always followed by a Progress Check.

## Materials

You are free to use whatever materials you have on hand to complete each of the exercises, but we suggest that you have the following materials available:

- Large sheets of paper
- Pens/pencils
- Scissors
- File folder
- Index cards
- Planning calendar

# Building a Contract With This Book

## What Will This Book Offer You?

We will invite you to complete a number of exercises and to answer some questions. We will take you on a carefully thought-out sequence of steps designed to help you ask and answer the six key questions for career and life management outlined earlier. We estimate a time commitment of approximately forty-eight hours to read the book and to complete the assignments. The amount of time will increase if you work with a partner or a group of people.

By now some goals, however hazy, might be forming in your head. Perhaps you are thinking—"I'll give it another few pages to see if this is the kind of thing I am interested in," or "It really might be useful to carry out some of the exercises." We invite you, therefore, to think carefully at this stage about just what you might want from a book on career and life management. To do this we want to introduce you to the concept of "contracting"—in itself a vital career and life management skill.

"Contracts" need not only be formal, written documents. They can be psychological contracts, too, which at some stage can be written down but not necessarily. Contracting is a process of clarifying objectives and making agreements. You can contract with a friend to go on vacation, with a spouse to divide up household tasks, or with a doctor to make some lifestyle changes. A contract usually involves two parties and requires you to be very specific about what you want, what you are prepared to do, and what you expect from the other party.

The advantage of conscious contracting, as opposed to half-formed or unexpressed expectations, is that it demands clarity of objectives, and as the poster says "If you don't know where you're going, you'll probably end up somewhere else." It also minimizes the possibilities of misunderstanding. We often experience and live with more problems than we need to because we do not "contract" clearly with people, organizations, and—yes—with ourselves!

It is possible to talk of making a contract with yourself, and that is exactly what we invite you to do if you are ready to commit yourself to career and life management right now. For some people contracting is really quite difficult, but we believe it is crucial. We offer you a contract on the following page. We invite you to complete this contract. You will be offered a chance to review it midway through the book. So, before reading any further, sit back, get comfortable, rid your mind of distractions, and answer the questions on the next page.

# CONTRACT

1. What do I really want to get from reading this book? Be as specific as possible.

2. What can I personally do to make sure that I get what I want?

3. Based on past experience, what can I do to avoid sabotaging myself, thereby not getting what I want? What can I do to prevent this?

4. How do I normally feel and behave if my expectations are not being met? How helpful is this for me? What can I do to ensure that my expectations will be met?

Signed by _____

Date _____

# QUESTION 1

# Who Am I?

We begin with you as you are now. But how accurate a representation is any snapshot—an arbitrary moment of frozen time? You need to know something of your history and get a perspective on your future. You are the living repository of your own history, shaped by it, influenced through it, and part creator of it. To begin, you must focus on the context of your life to date—the events, the experience, the peaks, the valleys, stresses sought and imposed, decisions made, decisions made for you, and the key people who populate your biography. What you have done, been, and learned so far will be your launching pad for the future.

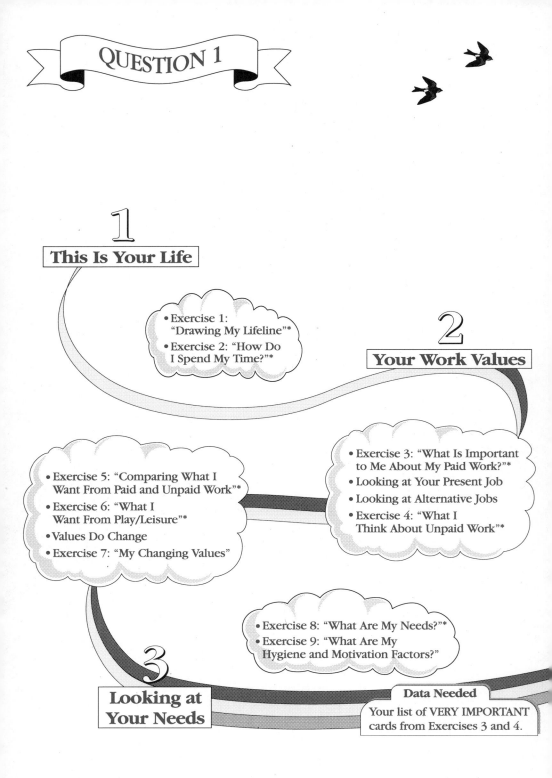

# QUESTION 1

## 1 This Is Your Life

- Exercise 1: "Drawing My Lifeline"*
- Exercise 2: "How Do I Spend My Time?"*

## 2 Your Work Values

- Exercise 3: "What Is Important to Me About My Paid Work?"*
- Looking at Your Present Job
- Looking at Alternative Jobs
- Exercise 4: "What I Think About Unpaid Work"*

- Exercise 5: "Comparing What I Want From Paid and Unpaid Work"*
- Exercise 6: "What I Want From Play/Leisure"*
- Values Do Change
- Exercise 7: "My Changing Values"

- Exercise 8: "What Are My Needs?"*
- Exercise 9: "What Are My Hygiene and Motivation Factors?"

## 3 Looking at Your Needs

### Data Needed

Your list of VERY IMPORTANT cards from Exercises 3 and 4.

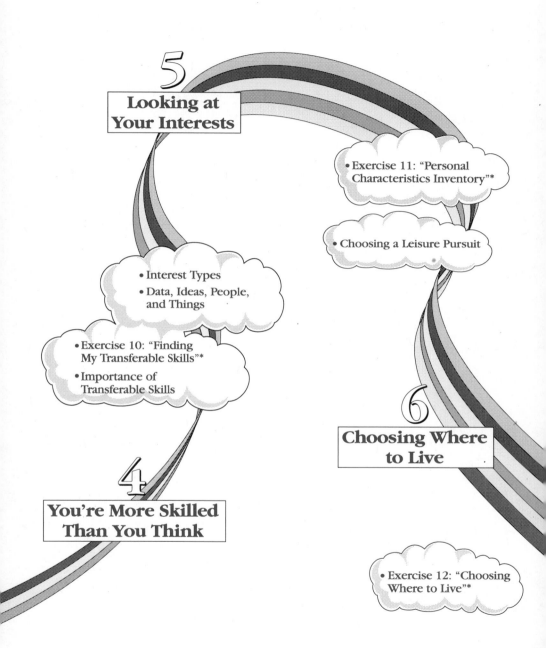

**5**
**Looking at Your Interests**

• Exercise 11: "Personal Characteristics Inventory"*

• Choosing a Leisure Pursuit

• Interest Types
• Data, Ideas, People, and Things

• Exercise 10: "Finding My Transferable Skills"*

• Importance of Transferable Skills

**6**
**Choosing Where to Live**

**4**
**You're More Skilled Than You Think**

• Exercise 12: "Choosing Where to Live"*

**\* = Essential Exercise**

# This Is Your Life

Reminder: Asterisked exercises are those we consider crucial to building your rainbows.

## Exercise 1: Drawing My Lifeline*

Rainbow Building Skill: Learn From Experience

- Take a very large sheet of paper and draw a line to represent your life. This might be a straight line, one with peaks and valleys, or even a spiral! You determine its shape.
- Indicate on the line where you are now with a large X.
- Write the key events or happenings in your life on the line, starting with events as early as you can remember and proceeding to the present. (The sample lifeline that follows is incomplete and only covers the first fifteen years of this person's life.)
- Leave plenty of space between the years. You will find that one memory triggers another, so be prepared to move back and forth along the line as the memories flow back to you.
- Now look back at each event and ask yourself the following questions, putting the appropriate symbol or symbols after each one. For some events none of the symbols may apply.

How stressful was it? Rate this on the scale:
S = somewhat stressful, SS = stressful, SSS = very stressful

| | |
|---|---|
| Was this a peak experience? | △ |
| Was this a valley experience? | ∪ |
| Was there important learning for me in this? | ! |
| Did I take a risk? | R |
| Did I choose to do this? | √ |
| Did I have no choice? | × |

Take as much time as you need to do this: This is your life!

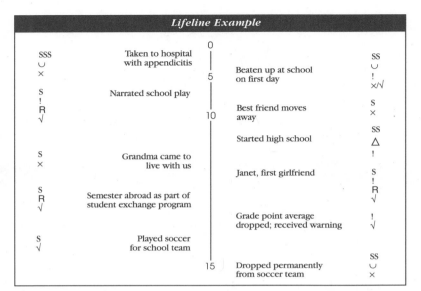

| | | | | |
|---|---|---|---|---|
| | | | **Lifeline Example** | |

SSS        Taken to hospital     0                          SS
∪           with appendicitis            Beaten up at school       ∪
×                         5    on first day                 !
                                                                  ×/√

*Transcription of the lifeline chart:*

- SSS ∪ × — Taken to hospital with appendicitis (age 0)
- Beaten up at school on first day (age 5) — SS ∪ ! ×/√
- S ! R √ — Narrated school play
- Best friend moves away (age 10) — S ×
- Started high school — SS △ !
- S × — Grandma came to live with us
- Janet, first girlfriend — S ! R √
- S R √ — Semester abroad as part of student exchange program
- Grade point average dropped; received warning — ! √
- S √ — Played soccer for school team
- Dropped permanently from soccer team (age 15) — SS ∪ ×

Next look at the following list of questions. Select those that are relevant or that provoke responses. Write down your answers and add any thoughts, ideas, or objectives that occur to you, and make a note of them in your "Aha!" folder.

What does this account of my life say about how I have lived my life so far?

Does anything surprise me?

What are the most important elements in my peak experiences?

What elements characterize the valleys or low points in my life? What have I learned (a) from my peak experiences? (b) from my low points?

Do I take risks? Are the results mostly positive or negative? Does my life divide into themes? What unfinished themes are there? Are there any changes in my life pattern with age?

- My life line
- Notes about my life so far

## Exercise 2: How Do I Spend My Time?*

Rainbow Building Skill: Know Yourself

What you have done so far is to step back and take a long look at your life as you have lived it up to now. The next step is to examine in greater detail just how you are investing your time right now. People will devote considerable time to analyzing return on investment or working out the best buy for an appliance, automobile, house, or brand of detergent, and yet do not apply the same time or skill to an analysis of their own lives.

- What returns am I getting for the time and energy I am expending?
- What parts of my life are "best buys"?
- How am I actually filling the hours of each day?

Memories of how we spend our time are notoriously unreliable. Weight control specialists have known for some time that asking people what they have eaten is very inaccurate. The only accurate way is to ask them to record what they do eat each day. We invite you to do the same with your use of time.

- Over one week keep a record of your activities. Begin on any day you like, but try to choose a fairly typical week and "log it."
- Record your activities at the end of each day or periodically throughout the day. A useful chart is provided on the next page, but if this breakdown into two-hour slots does not work for you, create your own. You will need a large sheet of paper.
- This is a crucial piece of data collection. You will be asked to refer back to it for Question 3: "How Satisfied Am I With Who and Where I Am?"
- This log will take you a week to complete, but you can continue with the other exercises, returning to this exercise when you have completed the log.

| Time Investment Record | | | | | | | | | | | | |
|---|---|---|---|---|---|---|---|---|---|---|---|---|
| | 2 | 4 | 6 | 8 | 10 | 12 | 2 | 4 | 6 | 8 | 10 | 12 |
| Mon. | | | | | | | | | | | | |
| Tues. | | | | | | | | | | | | |
| Wed. | | | | | | | | | | | | |
| Thurs. | | | | | | | | | | | | |
| Fri. | | | | | | | | | | | | |
| Sat. | | | | | | | | | | | | |
| Sun. | | | | | | | | | | | | |

When your record is complete, answer the following questions:

Is this week typical of my life? How is it atypical?

What does this "snapshot" reveal about the way I am currently spending my time?

How much of my week was spent doing things I choose to do?

Fill in the bar chart on the next page to indicate what percentage of time is spent in your different roles. (Some of your life roles will overlap so that your totals will probably be well over 100 percent.)

| Time Analysis Record | | | | | | | | | | |
|---|---|---|---|---|---|---|---|---|---|---|
| Percentage of Time Spent | | | | | | | | | | |
| Life Role | 10 | 20 | 30 | 40 | 50 | 60 | 70 | 80 | 90 | 100 |
| Child | | | | | | | | | | |
| Employee | | | | | | | | | | |
| Spouse | | | | | | | | | | |
| Parent | | | | | | | | | | |
| Citizen | | | | | | | | | | |
| Consumer | | | | | | | | | | |
| Friend | | | | | | | | | | |
| Pleasure seeker | | | | | | | | | | |
| Student | | | | | | | | | | |
| Homemaker | | | | | | | | | | |
| | | | | | | | | | | |
| | | | | | | | | | | |

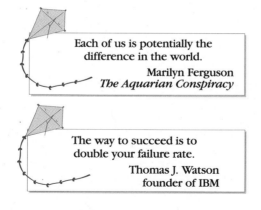

Each of us is potentially the difference in the world.

Marilyn Ferguson
*The Aquarian Conspiracy*

The way to succeed is to double your failure rate.

Thomas J. Watson
founder of IBM

Keep a Record

- My time investment record
- Notes about the way I use my time

# Rainbow Building Progress Check

Who Am I?

What have you learned about how you have been living your life up to now?

_____

_____

_____

_____

_____

_____

_____

_____

_____

_____

You reviewed your life and examined how you spend your time now. Collect data about key aspects of yourself. The next section will provide you with information about

- Values
- Interests
- Skills
- Where you want to live and work
- Life stage you are at now
- Career pattern desired

# Your Work Values

You are questioning your values whenever you ask

- "Where do I want to live and work?"
- "How do I like to spend my time?"
- "What kind of people do I choose to have around me?"
- "How important are money, status, autonomy, success, security, creativity, power, helping others, spontaneity, and risk taking?"

Being able to answer questions like these plays a key role in career and life management. The more you are able to live out your values, the more rewarding your life will be. In this section we will focus on what you value in work (paid and unpaid) and in play.

## Work Values

The following chart differentiates between paid work and unpaid work but acknowledges that we perform both kinds in our various life roles—child, homemaker, consumer, citizen, student, employee, spouse, parent, pleasure seeker, friend, etc.

| *Types of Work* | | |
| --- | --- | --- |
| | Liked | Disliked |
| Paid | A job in which the work is intrinsically rewarding. You might even do this for little or no pay. | A job involving work you would not choose to do unless you needed the money. |
| Unpaid | An activity you enjoy or feel is useful. You do it for no other reason. | Activities you do not enjoy but are obliged to do by force or contractual agreement. |

Work is

- An activity.
- A motivator that provides a sense of purpose and direction.
- A structure for living, although it might be regular or irregular.
- A source of identity and self-respect.
- A source of companions and friends.
- A factor in how other people see and feel about us.
- A source of money if someone wants to pay for what we can do.

We distinguish clearly between work and jobs. Real work is available for all of us, even if jobs are not. We must separate the issue of income from that of work. This is not to say that income is not important. It is of crucial importance to us all, and is a political issue demanding decisions from our society on how wealth should be distributed. Everyone needs work, everyone needs income, but not everyone can get a job, in the traditional sense, or wants one.

You may well ask: "What is wrong with equating work with a job?"

It is not so much that it is "wrong," but that the consequences of the link are increasingly misleading and a source of distress for many people. The person who is a full-time homemaker certainly works, but if those activities are not considered work, there is little status attached to it and the person can be discouraged from finding value in the work. Full-time parents are often regarded, and too often regard themselves, as unproductive. People who do not have a job at all are generally thought to be unproductive and can be the focus of considerable social criticism.

Work does not equal a job. It is far broader than that. Today, a job is typically seen as paid work involving a five-day week, seven to eight hours a day, with four weeks vacation. By the year AD 2000, work is likely to average thirty hours a week, include up to eight weeks annual vacation, and offer a bevy of employment alternatives incorporating job-sharing, flextime, telecommuting, industrial sabbaticals, a compressed work week, holding multiple jobs, and the gradual disappearance of the concept of "part-time" employment. It is only possible to have "part-time" employment if there is a consensus on what constitutes "full-time" employment.

Work ranges from activities that we like doing to those that we dislike doing. There is work that we are paid for and work for which we receive no direct financial reward.

## Types of Work

The concept of work is central to this book because work is central to each of us. An example may help to illustrate why definitions of work can vary so greatly. Let us examine the activity of gardening as it might appear to different people.

### Liked/Paid Work:

This person loves gardening for its own sake. It is a source of delight to her that she actually gets paid for it. It is her major source of income.

### Liked/Unpaid Work:

This person also loves gardening but either cannot get paid for doing it or would not choose to do it as his major source of income for a variety of reasons—he likes doing other things more, or it does not pay as much as he wants to earn. This activity has traditionally been labeled a leisure pursuit or a hobby.

### Disliked/Paid Work:

This person does not especially like gardening. If she did not have to earn money she would not choose to do it. She does it because there are no other jobs, or because she likes this better than the other available jobs.

### Disliked/Unpaid Work:

This person does not enjoy gardening. He has an arrangement with his wife, however, that he will do the gardening if she will do the housework as both agree that it needs to be done.

This scenario gets even more complicated when the work changes because the situation changes or because the person changes. For example, the disliked/unpaid work of gardening may only feel like that when you don't really have the time, the weather is disgusting, or you are sick. Similarly, as a result of having to garden, what began as a chore can sometimes be transformed into a pleasure as you discover new facets of your skills and personality.

## Exercise 3: What Is Important to Me About Paid Work?*

Rainbow Building Skills: Know Yourself, Make Decisions

- On the separate sheets marked "MY VALUE CARDS" (located in back of book) you will find cards to tear out and cut up. You should end up with a pack of 35 Work Value Cards and 5 Heading Cards. The Heading Cards, (in all capital letters) include the following:

> OF SOME IMPORTANCE
> NOT IMPORTANT
> QUITE IMPORTANT
> VERY IMPORTANT
> IMPORTANT

- Place the 5 heading cards in front of you as indicated below:

> Very Important
> Important
> Quite Important
> Of Some Importance
> Not Important

Look at each of the 35 Work Values Cards and ask yourself:
"How important is this aspect of work to me when I am considering paid work?"

- After sorting the cards into 5 columns, make certain that there are no more than 7 or 8 in the *Very Important* pile. If there are, you are not discriminating finely enough between the things that are important to you and we encourage you to reconsider your sort.
- If there are some important values for you not represented on the cards, create you own cards and add them to the sorting task.
- Rank order your *Very Important* cards from the most to the least important.

- Look at "My Paid Work Values" chart that follows and write in your rank-ordered *Very Important* work values in the lefthand column.
- Write in your *Not Important* cards in the space provided.

You now have a tool you can use to analyze the suitability of any paid work prospect (including your present job if you have one). In a moment you will analyze your unpaid work values.

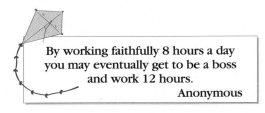

By working faithfully 8 hours a day you may eventually get to be a boss and work 12 hours.

Anonymous

## Looking at Your Present Job

Ask yourself this question about each of your *Very Important* work values:

  Does my present job allow me to satisfy this value?

Rank each value on a 1 to 10 scale with 1 = never satisfies and 10 = totally satisfies.

Fill in your scores in the _____ space on the chart.

You will see that a weight for your answers has already been filled in for you. Simply complete the calculations. For example:

6 x 8 = 48
8 x 7 = 56
2 x 6 = 12

The columns for Job Alternatives will be explained later.

| My Paid Work Values | | | |
|---|---|---|---|
| Very Important | My Present Job | Job Alternative #1 | Job Alternative #2 |
| 1. | __ x 8 = | __ x 8 = | __ x 8 = |
| 2. | __ x 7 = | __ x 7 = | __ x 7 = |
| 3. | __ x 6 = | __ x 6 = | __ x 6 = |
| 4. | __ x 5 = | __ x 5 = | __ x 5 = |
| 5. | __ x 4 = | __ x 4 = | __ x 4 = |
| 6. | __ x 3 = | __ x 3 = | __ x 3 = |
| 7. | __ x 2 = | __ x 2 = | __ x 2 = |
| 8. | __ x 1 = | __ x 1 = | __ x 1 = |
| | Total = | Total = | Total = |

My Not Important Cards

| | |
|---|---|
| 1. | |
| 2. | |
| 3. | |
| 4. | Check any of these that are features of your present job or any alternative jobs |
| 5. | |
| 6. | |
| 7. | |
| 8. | |

Add up the total for your present job. If you give 10 points for each of your 8 Very Important values, your maximum total would be 360, although it is highly unlikely that anyone would achieve 360.

Answer the following questions:

Overall, how much opportunity is there in my present job for expression or these values?

Do any of the values in my *Not Important* column feature in my present job?

Do I find opportunities to satisfy my values outside of my job?

Can I think of any jobs (other than my present one) that would closely fit my key values?

Are my work values different now than at other times in my life? In what ways?

Can I think of any objectives I would like to set as a result of this exercise?

## Looking at Alternative Jobs

If you don't have a job and want one, or if you have a job but are actively considering other jobs, Exercise 4 will help provide some focus. In addition, fill in your answers for as many alternative jobs as you are considering. Total up the scores for each job separately, scoring each one on how it might provide an outlet for your work values.

How do the jobs compare in the scoring? Does this feel right? If not, why not?

Do any of the jobs contain any of my *Not Important* characteristics?

Do I need additional information before making a choice? If so, what information?

Do I need to set any objectives?

By the year 2000, three out of every four workers currently employed will need retraining for the new jobs of the next century.

- "My Paid Work Values" chart
- Notes about what I've discovered
- Objectives I should pursue

## Exercise 4: What I Think About Unpaid Work*

Rainbow Building Skills: Know Yourself, Set Objectives

- List examples of the kinds of unpaid work that you do in your life on the "My Unpaid Work Values" chart.

For example: clean the house, baby-sit, church duties, "do-it-yourself" activities, garden, cook, keep accounts for a club, organize outings for old people, wash clothes, etc.

- Sort the cards into columns under the five headings by asking yourself the question:

### What is important to me in unpaid work?

- Rank order them.
- Write down your *Very Important* and *Not Important* cards.
- Use the "My Unpaid Work Values" chart on the next page. Write in the activities you wish to analyze.

| My Unpaid Work Values | | | | |
|---|---|---|---|---|
| Very Important | Activity Number 1 | Activity Number 2 | Activity Number 3 | Activity Number 4 |
| 1. | __ x 8 = | __ x 8 = | __ x 8 = | __ x 8 = |
| 2. | __ x 7 = | __ x 7 = | __ x 7 = | __ x 7 = |
| 3. | __ x 6 = | __ x 6 = | __ x 6 = | __ x 6 = |
| 4. | __ x 5 = | __ x 5 = | __ x 5 = | __ x 5 = |
| 5. | __ x 4 = | __ x 4 = | __ x 4 = | __ x 4 = |
| 6. | __ x 3 = | __ x 3 = | __ x 3 = | __ x 3 = |
| 7. | __ x 2 = | __ x 2 = | __ x 2 = | __ x 2 = |
| 8. | __ x 1 = | __ x 1 = | __ x 1 = | __ x 1 = |
| | Total = | Total = | Total = | Total = |

| My Not Important Cards | |
|---|---|
| 1. | |
| 2. | |
| 3. | |
| 4. | Check any of these that are factors in your unpaid work activities |
| 5. | |
| 6. | |
| 7. | |
| 8. | |

How do my unpaid work activities compare in the scoring? Does this feel right? If not, why not?

Do any of my unpaid work activities contain any of my *Not Important* values?

Do I need to set any objectives?

- "My Unpaid Work Values" chart
- Notes about what I've discovered
- Objectives I should pursue

## Exercise 5: Comparing What I Want From Paid and Unpaid Work*

Rainbow Building Skill: Know Yourself

- Complete the card sort for paid work as described previously.
- Complete the card sort for unpaid work.

Are there any differences between my *Very Important* cards for paid and unpaid work? What are they?

Any differences between my *Not Important* cards for paid and unpaid work?

- You might like to compare your analysis with the following one.

### *Bill Charlton*

Below are Bill's sortings of his paid and unpaid work values.

| Paid Work | | | | |
|---|---|---|---|---|
| Very Important | Important | Quite Important | Of Some Importance | Not Important |
| Independence Creativity Money Communication Learning Friendship Excitement Time freedom Being expert | Artistic Well-known organization Fast pace Recognition Decision making | Help society Variety Place of work Challenge Risk Status Persuading people Help others Work with others | Work alone Promotion Contact with people Pressure Competition | Precise work Routine Community Physical challenge Security Peace Supervision |

| Unpaid Work | | | | |
|---|---|---|---|---|
| Very Important | Important | Quite Important | Of Some Importance | Not Important |
| Creativity<br>Artistic<br>Helping others<br>Communication<br>Friendship<br>Time freedom<br>Independence<br>Place of work<br>Physical challenge | Work with others<br>Money<br>Status | Peaceful<br>Work alone<br>Learning<br>Help society<br>Challenge | Contact with people<br>Being expert<br>Decision making<br>Persuading people<br>Risk<br>Precise work | Community<br>Routine<br>Promotion<br>Supervision<br>Fast pace<br>Recognition<br>Security<br>Competition<br>Well-known organization<br>Pressure |

Bill said,

"From this example it is clear that I have some values that are important to me for any work I do, whether paid or unpaid—creativity, independence, friendship, time freedom, communication. This exercise highlights just how crucial these needs are to me as a total person. I know what my overriding work needs are. I also know that my unpaid work needs to compensate for what I don't require as much from in my paid work, e.g., artistic and physical challenge."

## Exercise 6: What I Want From Play/Leisure*

Rainbow Building Skill: Know Yourself

- Do the card sort again, this time asking yourself: What is important to me for play and leisure activities?
- Write down the eight most important play values in the spaces provided on the "Play Values" chart below.
- Write down your four favorite play or leisure activities in the spaces provided.
- Ask yourself for each activity how far your play values are being satisfied (1 = never, 10 = totally)
- Write in your *Not Important* play values on the chart.

| My Play Values | | | | |
|---|---|---|---|---|
| Very Important | Play #1 | Play #2 | Play #3 | Play #4 |
| 1. | __ x 8 = | __ x 8 = | __ x 8 = | __ x 8 = |
| 2. | __ x 7 = | __ x 7 = | __ x 7 = | __ x 7 = |
| 3. | __ x 6 = | __ x 6 = | __ x 6 = | __ x 6 = |
| 4. | __ x 5 = | __ x 5 = | __ x 5 = | __ x 5 = |
| 5. | __ x 4 = | __ x 4 = | __ x 4 = | __ x 4 = |
| 6. | __ x 3 = | __ x 3 = | __ x 3 = | __ x 3 = |
| 7. | __ x 2 = | __ x 2 = | __ x 2 = | __ x 2 = |
| 8. | __ x 1 = | __ x 1 = | __ x 1 = | __ x 1 = |
| | Total = | Total = | Total = | Total = |

My Not Important Cards

| | |
|---|---|
| 1. | |
| 2. | |
| 3. | |
| 4. | Check if they feature in your play activities. |
| 5. | |
| 6. | |
| 7. | |
| 8. | |

## Bill Charlton

Bill's play values are also reproduced.

| Play Values | | | | |
|---|---|---|---|---|
| Very Important | Important | Quite Important | Of Some Importance | Not Important |
| Independence Peaceful Place I am Creativity Physical challenge Being alone Time freedom Learning | Variety Excitement Communication Routine Recognition Fast pace | Friendship Artistic Competition Security Challenge Being with others Work alone | Contact with people Precise work Community Help society Help others | Pressure Being expert Supervision Decision making Well-known organization Persuading people Status Money |

Bill said,

"This again underlies my central need for independence, creativity, and time freedom in all I do. It also shows how a balance between work and play is important to me, i.e., I enjoy physical challenge and competition when playing soccer and other games. I also don't want status, money, decision making, supervision, and persuading people to have any place in my play activities.

"There is also a contrast in that my play activities must encompass both peace and physical challenge, which for me means lying in the sun reading and a hard game of soccer.

"Doing the exercise made me realize just how little time I had in my life for play and that is a thought for my 'Aha!' folder."

- Notes about what I've discovered
- What I've discovered about my values

## Values Do Change

Our values are a mirror image of who we are at any moment. Perhaps more dramatically we would argue that we are merely the mirror images of our values—so central are they as the "drivers" behind our life journeys. Periodically, however, those journeys change directions as a result of life events, growing older, and our changing views of ourselves. There is nothing unusual about that. On the contrary, there would be something more unusual if our values stayed constant.

### Exercise 7: My Changing Values

Rainbow Building Skills: Know Yourself, Learn From Experience

You have already sorted the values cards for what is important to you now. Do the following additional card sorts for paid work only.

- No. 1: Sort them as if you were 18.
- No. 2: Sort them as if you were 30.
- No. 3: Sort them as if you were 45.
- No. 4: Sort them as if you were 65.

For some of these sortings, you may be projecting into the future.

What changes am I aware of? What does this say about me?

What has stayed constant? What does this say?

What does this say about how I see my future?

(Record your answers to this in your "Aha!" folder. It will be useful data for Question 4: What Changes Do I Want?)

Values and needs also change as a result of how successful we are in satisfying them! Let us illuminate that curious statement. Abraham Maslow was a psychologist who said that we must view human needs in a hierarchical way. By that he meant that our needs can be arranged in an order, some of which have to be satisfied before we can or want to address ourselves to a higher level of need.

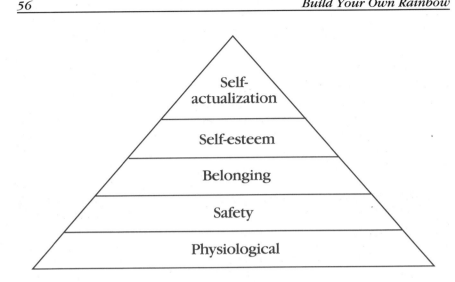

The diagram demonstrates this. From this it is clear that if your main concern is getting an income just to keep yourself alive, you are unlikely to be spending much time wondering about the cosmic importance of your place in the universe! It also follows that at certain periods of your life you may revert to a lower level of need, for example, if you suddenly become unemployed or lose a spouse. This readjustment of your needs should not in itself be a cause for concern. This reaction is a normal response to events such as these. It does not mean that in some way you have regressed.

Notes about what I've discovered

If work were a good thing, the rich
would have found a way of keeping
it all to themselves.
                        Haitian proverb

The growth occupations are in healthcare, electronics, security, banking, insurance, professional and scientific services, and adult education.

# Looking at Your Needs

## Exercise 8: What Are My Needs?*

Rainbow Building Skill: Know Yourself

Your values, simply, are an expression of your needs. This exercise will give you an opportunity to discover where you are on Maslow's levels-of-needs diagram. One thing you will discover is that you are unlikely to find that you are living totally at one level of need.

On the back of some of the "My Values Cards" are printed the following words: "Having," "Doing," and "Being." These cards represent examples of the needs in the hierarchy. Our physiological and safety needs can be grouped together as indicating things we *Have* to have before we can focus on anything else. Our belonging and self-esteem needs indicate what we need to *Do* before we feel free to begin to *Be* the kind of person we can be. The latter represents our self-actualization needs, which is where we strive to reach our full potential, unencumbered by material and social needs.

Look at your eight or so *Very Important* cards. How many of them are Having, Doing, or Being cards?

The following cards represent each area of need.

| Having | Doing | Being |
|---|---|---|
| Security | Work with others | Learning |
| Money | Community | Independence |
| Routine | Friendship | Creativity |
| Peace | Contact with people | Challenge |
| | Recognition | Help society |
| | Being expert | Risk |
| | Promotion | |
| | Status | |

What does my card sorting tell me about my hierarchy of needs?

Am I primarily at one level or are my needs distributed throughout the levels?

What does this say about who I am now?

How might I like to be different?

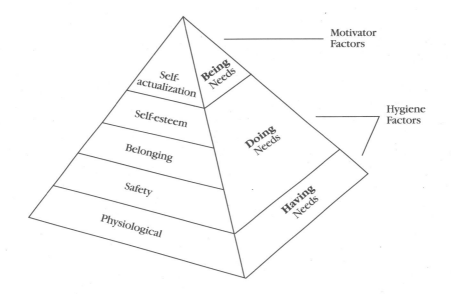

The diagram above sums up what we have been discussing about levels of needs and has added to it an important idea developed from behavioral scientist Frederick Herzberg. Although originally concerned with paid work only, we believe his theory can apply to unpaid work too. He discovered that what made employees dissatisfied was not always the opposite of what brought them satisfaction. For example, he found that people could get very dissatisfied with problems about salary, job security, supervisor behavior, and company policy. However, when these were rectified it did not automatically guarantee satisfaction. That only derived from factors present in the job, for example, achievement, recognition, and growth.

Herzberg called the first group "Hygiene" factors, because they helped to prevent dissatisfaction but in themselves would never provide real satisfaction. In other words, you can be getting a good salary in a secure job in a company you like and not feel dissatisfied, but not feel satisfied either. For that you need some of the "Motivator" elements to be present.

## Exercise 9: What Are My Hygiene and Motivation Factors?

Rainbow Building Skill: Know Yourself

Some researchers have criticized Herzberg saying that it is naive to assume that what is a motivator for one person will be a motivator for everyone, for example, increasing responsibility. Although this criticism might be true, it need not diminish the value of the theory. This exercise will enable you to work out for yourself what are your own Hygiene and Motivator factors. You will look at these again in Section 3.

- Sort through the "My Values Cards." Ask yourself these two questions:
1. "Which of these causes me irritation or frustration if I don't have them?"
2. "Which of these, when I do have them, makes me feel really fulfilled and involved with my work?"

Now sort the cards into two piles, according to your answers.

- Write down your answers from your cards.

   List 1 represents your Hygiene factors.

   List 2 represents your Motivator factors.

 Does this suggest anything for my "Aha!" folder?

 Notes about what I've discovered

# Rainbow Building Progress Check

## Who Am I?

What have you learned about your values and needs and how they might change?

_____

_____

_____

_____

_____

_____

_____

_____

Having looked at what is important to you (your values), the next question is focused on what you can do well—your abilities or skills. Many people have difficulty in identifying their skills. Part of this difficulty reflects growing up in a culture that deals harshly with people who brag, are immodest, or are too self-important. Because of this, many people are more skilled in describing what they are poor at than what they are good at! But, culture not withstanding, we are also not skilled at knowing how to identify the broad range of things we can do well. This is a vital career planning skill. It is essential to know the base of skills on which you can build changes in your lifestyle or career.

# You're More Skilled Than You Think

## Importance of Transferable Skills

One reason why we are poor at identifying our skills can be traced to the paramount importance of the paid worker role in our lives. Skills are often linked to the jobs we do. Because we are technicians, accountants, social workers, etc., we find it relatively easy to see that we have skills in working with electronics, or knowledge of bookkeeping systems, or an understanding of how court orders should be followed up. However, it is often more difficult to dig deeper than these job content skills to discover the underlying skills that are transferable—not only to a variety of other jobs, but also to other life roles. This concept was pioneered by Bernard Haldane in his work with people returning to the civilian work force after World War II.

For example, many of you may have worked at one time as a salesperson. But it would not be unusual to hear someone who had actually been a salesperson for much of his or her working life, when asked what skills they have, reply with a statement like "None—I've only been a salesperson." This is because they can see no deeper than the job content skills. In the table that follows, we see the job content skills for a salesperson in the left-hand column and the underlying transferable skills in the other columns defined under Data, People, Things, and Ideas. We chose salesperson because it seems like a relatively straightforward job and it can convey the idea of what we are looking for in this exercise. An awareness of the transferable skills involved in the jobs/roles you have been doing might help you make some changes in your career, without necessarily requiring much—or even any—retraining.

There is an increasing move toward working from home. Surveys indicate that nearly a quarter of the work force does at least some work out of their homes. There is a growing trend, particularly in the computer field toward "telecommuting"— working for a corporation from the home connected by telephone, fax, and often modem.

| Skills—*"None, I've Only Been a Salesperson."* | | | | |
|---|---|---|---|---|
| Job Content Skills | Work With Data | Work With People | Work With Things | Work With Ideas |
| Set up merchandise displays and sales tags | Understand and apply sale charts | Make people feel welcome and excited about the merchandise | Manipulate items rapidly and artistically | Think of new display layouts |
| Give information about products, find items to fit specific needs | Explain product qualities, ability to memorize | Help and inform | Show how items work or coordinate | Create new uses for items and ways to coordinate them |
| Take special orders | Write clearly to be understood by others; look up codes, prices, etc. | Check for understanding, maintain relationships, make customers feel special, work with venders | Use catalogues, order forms | Think of new products to stock or times to stock them |
| Write and file orders or input them on a computer system | Communicate information to others | Interact with people in warehouse, receiving, shipping, etc., contact customers for follow-up | Use office systems, telephone, computer, etc. | Think of new order systems |
| Package items for customers | Know policies for gift wrappinig, boxing, bagging, or prepping merchandise | Help customers pick out packaging and make merchandise easy for them to take | Balance items, add promotional materials, pack, wrap, or unwrap items | Create improved ways to protect, decorate, or transport merchandise |

| Skills—"None, I've Only Been a Salesperson." (continued) | | | | |
|---|---|---|---|---|
| Job Content Skills | Work With Data | Work With People | Work With Things | Work With Ideas |
| Suggest additional items or accessories | Ability to memorize | Persuade | Demonstrate improved uses or aesthetics | Think of every possible need associated with the product and new services to offer |
| Ring up items, take money, and provide change | Work with money, and credit card, check, and financing procedures | Deal with people courteously, help them understand prices | Manipulate cash and register or calculator | Find ways to accommodate how the customer would like to pay |
| Thank customers and check on satisfaction | Seek feedback, remember names and other personal facts about customers | Listen, care, deal with people courteously, and make them feel special and appreciated | Give out and collect customer surveys, help with packages | Find solutions to negative customer experiences |

## Exercise 10: Finding My Transferable Skills*

Rainbow Building Skills: Know Yourself, Research Skills

In the back of the book, the pages labeled "SKILLS DESCRIPTIONS," are a number of cards to cut out, as you did with "MY VALUES CARDS."

- Among the cards you cut out will be 4 cards with the following capitalized words on them:
  - VERY COMPETENT
  - COMPETENT
  - ADEQUATE FOR TASK
  - UNDEVELOPED
- Place these 4 cards in front of you. Sort all the rest among the 4 catagories by asking yourself:

Which of these skills can I perform very competently, competently, adequately, and which have I not yet developed?

- If you believe you have some transferable skills that are not represented on the cards, write on the blank cards provided. In the following table, "My Transferable Skills," write down all of the skills for which you assess yourself as *Very Competent* and *Competent.*
- Look at the skills in the *Competent, Adequate for Task,* and *Undeveloped* piles. Which of these would you like to develop? Write these down in the table.
- Take your *Very Competent* and *Competent* skills and sort them into three piles indicating those you:
                    Want to Use a Great Deal
                    Want to Use Sometimes
                    Want to Use Rarely or Never
- The skills you have identified as your *Very Competent* ones and *Want to Use a Great Deal* are your most transferable skills.
- The skills you have identified as your *Competent* and *Want to Use Sometimes* are your next most transferable skills.

  Not wanting to use these skills does not necessarily make them nontransferable. But people are unlikely to want to look for opportunities that involve using skills they are less motivated to use.

- Each of the skill cards has a letter on them: D, I, P, or T.

## Data, Ideas, People, and Things

*D = Data.* These represent the kind of skills required to record, communicate, evaluate, and organize facts or data about goods and services. People who like using these skills typically enjoy working with figures, systems, and routines.

*I = Ideas.* These represent skills used in being creative, designing conceptual models and systems, and experimenting with words, figures, and music. People who like using these skills typically enjoy creating, discovering, interpreting, synthesizing, and abstract thinking.

*P = People.* These represent skills used in helping, informing, teaching, serving, persuading, entertaining, motivating, selling, and directing other people. People who use these skills like to work for changes in other people's behavior.

*T = Things.* These represent skills used in making, repairing, transporting, and servicing. People with these skills like using tools and machinery and understanding how things work.

 How many of my transferable skills are in each of the categories Data, Ideas, People, Things?

Add these letters to the following "My Transferable Skills" table.
Place D, I, P, or T after each skill.

| My Transferable Skills | | | |
|---|---|---|---|
| Very Competent | Competent | Want to Use a Great Deal | Skills I Would Like to Develop |
| | | | |
| | | Want to Use Sometimes | |
| | | | |
| | | Want to Use Rarely or Never | |
| | | | |

Women hold less than 5 percent of the executive seats in American corporations even though they represent 47 percent of the work force.

Males today average 4.5 years on a job and females average 3.8 years.

About 43 percent of families have two wage earners.

As a result of falling birth rates in the late 1960's and early 1970's, the labor force is hardly growing at all. Thus, most of the newly jobless are people who have been working for some time and, consequently, have more to lose.

- My transferable skills chart
- My position on the map
- List of suggested jobs

## Interest Types

Your interests represent your preferences for doing some activities instead of others. Some people like driving cars, others like exploring caves, some like keeping financial records, while others like drawing diagrams.

### Things Focus

You like to work with tools, objects, machines, or animals. You like to develop manual, mechanical, agricultural, and electronic skills and prefer jobs that involve building and repairing things. You like using your hands. You are more gifted physically than intellectually. You admire physical coordination, strength, agility, and logic. You like being outdoors and dealing with concrete problems. You tend to be down to earth and matter of fact. You solve problems by *Doing*.

## Ideas Focus

You enjoy using your mind and tend to be curious, studious, independent, intellectual, sometimes unconventional, and introspective. You like to develop skills in mathematics, biology, and the physical sciences and prefer scientific and medical jobs. You like thinking through problems, trusting your own mind more than other people and things. You admire logic, use insight, enjoy intellectual challenges. You solve problems by *Thinking*.

## Ideas and People Focus

You like to feel free from routine. You like to develop skills in language, art, music, drama, and writing. You trust your mind, body, and feelings and are suspicious of things. You enjoy beauty, unstructured activity, variety, interesting and unusual sounds, sights, textures, and people. You tend to be creative, talented, and freewheeling, often nonconformist, sensitive, independent, introspective, and expressive. You like jobs where you can use your creative skills. You solve problems by being *Creative*.

## People Focus

You live through your feelings. Relying on gut reactions, you like activities that involve informing, training, teaching, understanding, and helping others. You develop skills for working with people. You tend to be helpful, friendly, a concerned leader, sensitive, supportive, responsible, perceptive, genuine, tactful, and empathetic. You enjoy being close to people, sharing problems, being in charge, and participating in unstructured activities. You like jobs such as teaching, nursing, and counseling. You solve problems by using *Feelings*.

## People and Data Focus

You love projects. You like leading and influencing people, are often ambitious, outgoing, energetic, self-confident, independent, enthusiastic, sensitive, and logical. You develop skills to lead, motivate, and persuade people. You enjoy organizing, managing, variety, status, power, and money. You solve problems by taking *Risks*.

## Data and Things Focus

You enjoy orderliness and clear routines. You like activities that encourage organizing information in a clear and logical way. You tend to be responsible, dependable, careful, logical, and accurate. You have an eye for detail. You enjoy order, security, and certainty, and identify with power and status. You develop office and mathemetical skills. You like jobs involving systems or operating computers and word processors. Often you like working in large organizations. You solve problems by following *Routines.*

Next turn to the following World of Employment Map to see all areas of employment located there. Jobs have been assigned to 28 Job Families. A Job Family is a group of jobs related to one another on the basis of their degree of involvement in working with Data, Ideas, People, and Things. The 28 Job Families are described in Appendix 1.

- Examine the World of Employment Map. The interest type(s) above correspond to four regions: Data, People, Ideas, and Things. Within each region are Job Families where people with your kinds of interest tend to cluster.

- For a more direct reading of which jobs might be suitable for you according to your interests, look up a specific Job Family in Appendix 1. Families are arranged in alphabetical order. Job Families are subdivided into broad job subgroupings, which in turn list specific jobs.

- Each Job Family also includes a range of courses that require similar skills or that attract people with similar interests. See The World of Education Map and Appendix 2 to identify education courses that might correspond to your skills and interests.

# *World of Employment Map*

## T H I N G S

| Building Maintenance | Agriculture, Forestry, & Fishery |
| Construction | Electricity & Electronics |
| Food Processing | Timber Products |
| Textile & Apparel | Metal Working |
| Transportation | Mining |
| Mechanical | Other Production |

## D A T A

Clerical

Bookkeeping & Accounting

Engineering & Design

Science & Laboratory

Inventory Control

## I D E A S

Graphic Arts

Social Research & Planning

Arts & Entertainment

Mathematics & Computing

Literary

Administrative

Sales

Food Service

Health Service

Protective Service

Legal, Educational, & Social Services

## P E O P L E

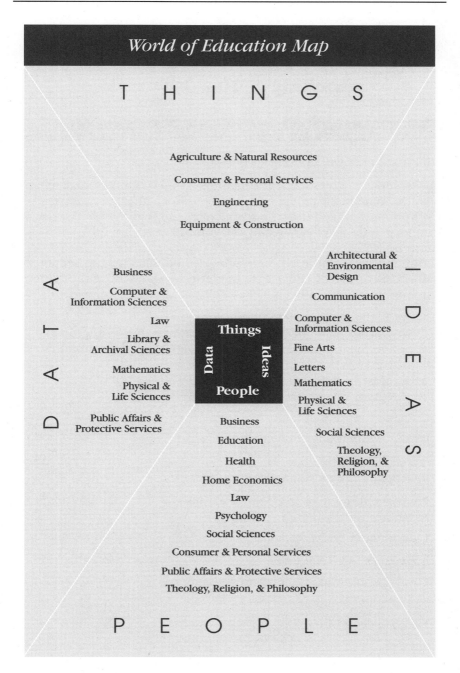

World of Education Map

THINGS

Agriculture & Natural Resources

Consumer & Personal Services

Engineering

Equipment & Construction

DATA

Business

Computer &
Information Sciences

Law

Library &
Archival Sciences

Mathematics

Physical &
Life Sciences

Public Affairs &
Protective Services

Things
Data   Ideas
People

Architectural &
Environmental
Design

Communication

Computer &
Information Sciences

Fine Arts

Letters

Mathematics

Physical &
Life Sciences

Social Sciences

Theology,
Religion, &
Philosophy

IDEAS

Business

Education

Health

Home Economics

Law

Psychology

Social Sciences

Consumer & Personal Services

Public Affairs & Protective Services

Theology, Religion, & Philosophy

PEOPLE

# Looking at Your Interests

## Exercise 11: Personal Characteristics Inventory

Rainbow Building Skill: Know Yourself

This inventory gives you information about your personal characteristics. Some items reflect concrete behavior, other items are traits or descriptions, and still others are statements of belief or value. Use the inventory to discover how you view yourself *now*, not how you would like to be.

Directions: As you read each item, decide whether the sentence is true or descriptive of you. Circle the letter to the right of the sentence that most accurately reflects your decision.

N = Not at all, definitely untrue for me.
O = Occasionally this is true of me (at least 25% of the time).
F = Frequently this is an accurate description of me (about 50% of the time).
M = Most of the time this would be descriptive of me.
H = Highly characteristic, definitely true for me.

| | | | | | |
|---|---|---|---|---|---|
| 1. I meet the needs of other people. | N | O | F | M | H |
| 2. I have fun. | N | O | F | M | H |
| 3. Respecting others is important to me. | N | O | F | M | H |
| 4. My perception of people and situations is accurate. | N | O | F | M | H |
| 5. I know what my biases are. | N | O | F | M | H |
| 6. I like to be a playful child. | N | O | F | M | H |
| 7. Loyalty to my friends is important to me. | N | O | F | M | H |
| 8. My daily life is full of surprises. | N | O | F | M | H |
| 9. I do not need other people. | N | O | F | M | H |

10. Class distinctions are unimportant to me.    N O F M H

11. I am a responsible person.    N O F M H

12. I like to share myself with others.    N O F M H

13. I can see the humorous side of serious matters.    N O F M H

14. I express my anger clearly and directly.    N O F M H

15. I accept my strengths.    N O F M H

16. I avoid doing what I believe is wrong.    N O F M H

17. I strive to keep my life simple and natural.    N O F M H

18. I am rarely lonely.    N O F M H

19. I enjoy my own absurdity.    N O F M H

20. Racial and national differences interest me.    N O F M H

21. Every day is different for me.    N O F M H

22. I delight in learning new things.    N O F M H

23. I can give to others and expect no return.    N O F M H

24. Nothing is routine for me.    N O F M H

25. I think clearly.    N O F M H

26. I believe the end never justifies the means.    N O F M H

27. I can tolerate chaos and disorder.    N O F M H

28. Working toward a goal is more enjoyable than attaining it.    N O F M H

29. I am amused by much of what I experience.    N O F M H

30. I like to be myself.    N O F M H

31. I am untroubled by problems with authority.    N O F M H

32. I experience no pressure to conform to social norms.    N O F M H

33. I accept my limitations.    N O F M H

34. The meaning of life is clear to me.    N O F M H

35. I enjoy discussing philosophical issues.    N O F M H

36. I know the difference between what I want and what I need.    N O F M H

37. I tolerate other peoples' failings and shortcomings.                    N  O  F  M  H

38. My life has a definite purpose.                                         N  O  F  M  H

39. My major satisfactions come from within.                               N  O  F  M  H

40. I can let go of my own interests.                                       N  O  F  M  H

41. Art, music, and beautiful things strengthen and enrich me.             N  O  F  M  H

42. I believe that supernatural phenomena occur.                           N  O  F  M  H

43. I see the positive side of things.                                     N  O  F  M  H

44. I can make myself at home anywhere.                                    N  O  F  M  H

45. I have had experiences when I lost my sense of space and time.         N  O  F  M  H

46. I am my own person.                                                     N  O  F  M  H

47. I am aware of the mysterious aspect of life.                           N  O  F  M  H

48. Achievement is less important to me than contentment.                  N  O  F  M  H

49. I am rarely self-conscious.                                            N  O  F  M  H

50. Empathy comes easily for me.                                           N  O  F  M  H

51. I can let things happen without planning.                             N  O  F  M  H

52. I do original work.                                                     N  O  F  M  H

53. I know the pain and joy of closeness.                                  N  O  F  M  H

54. I prize the dignity of all persons.                                    N  O  F  M  H

55. I am patient with others.                                              N  O  F  M  H

56. I like to be sexually close with others.                              N  O  F  M  H

57. I am an uninhibited person.                                            N  O  F  M  H

58. Dress and style are unimportant to me.                                N  O  F  M  H

59. I have definite moral standards.                                       N  O  F  M  H

60. I take good care of myself.                                            N  O  F  M  H

61. I learn something new every day.                                       N  O  F  M  H

62. I am excited by experimentation and risk taking.                      N  O  F  M  H

63. I believe all human beings are members of one big family.   N O F M H

64. My actions are based on my choices, not needs.   N O F M H

65. I rarely censor my thoughts.   N O F M H

66. I can disengage myself from petty concerns.   N O F M H

67. I am a spiritual person (though not necessarily religious).   N O F M H

68. I am rarely defensive.   N O F M H

69. I learn from many different places and persons.   N O F M H

70. I am never bored.   N O F M H

71. I am at ease with cultural traditions different from my own.   N O F M H

72. I have intense inner experiences.   N O F M H

73. Determining what is real and what is phony is easy for me.   N O F M H

74. I am objective about most things.   N O F M H

75. I feel kinship with most people I meet.   N O F M H

## Scoring

Transfer your letter responses from the inventory to each of the following fifteen scales and write in the value for each response.

N = -2
O = -1
F = 0
M = +1
H = +2

Add the values of the items in each scale for a score.

## Scale

### 1. Efficient Reality Perception

| Items | | | | | |
|---|---|---|---|---|---|
| | 4 | 25 | 27 | 36 | 73 |
| Letter | | | | | |
| Value | | | | | |
| Score | | | | | |

### 2. Acceptance of Self, Others, Human Nature

| Items | | | | | |
|---|---|---|---|---|---|
| | 15 | 33 | 37 | 60 | 68 |
| Letter | | | | | |
| Value | | | | | |
| Score | | | | | |

### 3. Spontaneity, Simplicity, Naturalness

| Items | | | | | |
|---|---|---|---|---|---|
| | 17 | 24 | 48 | 51 | 65 |
| Letter | | | | | |
| Value | | | | | |
| Score | | | | | |

### 4. Problem Centeredness

| Items | | | | | |
|---|---|---|---|---|---|
| | 1 | 35 | 38 | 40 | 49 |
| Letter | | | | | |
| Value | | | | | |
| Score | | | | | |

### 5. Detachment and Privacy

| Items | | | | | |
|---|---|---|---|---|---|
| | 9 | 18 | 30 | 66 | 74 |
| Letter | | | | | |
| Value | | | | | |
| Score | | | | | |

### 6. Autonomy and Independence of Culture and Environments

| Items | | | | | |
|---|---|---|---|---|---|
| | 32 | 39 | 44 | 46 | 64 |
| Letter | | | | | |
| Value | | | | | |
| Score | | | | | |

## 7. Freshness of Appreciation

| Items | | | | | |
|---|---|---|---|---|---|
| | 21 | 41 | 43 | 61 | 70 |
| Letter | | | | | |
| Value | | | | | |
| Score | | | | | |

## 8. Capacity for Peak Experiences

| Items | | | | | |
|---|---|---|---|---|---|
| | 42 | 45 | 47 | 67 | 72 |
| Letter | | | | | |
| Value | | | | | |
| Score | | | | | |

## 9. *Gemeinschaftsgefuhl*

| Items | | | | | |
|---|---|---|---|---|---|
| | 23 | 50 | 54 | 63 | 75 |
| Letter | | | | | |
| Value | | | | | |
| Score | | | | | |

## 10. Interpersonal Relations

| Items | | | | | |
|---|---|---|---|---|---|
| | 7 | 12 | 53 | 55 | 56 |
| Letter | | | | | |
| Value | | | | | |
| Score | | | | | |

## 11. Democratic Character Structure

| Items | | | | | |
|---|---|---|---|---|---|
| | 3 | 5 | 10 | 11 | 14 |
| Letter | | | | | |
| Value | | | | | |
| Score | | | | | |

## 12. Ethical Standards

| Items | | | | | |
|---|---|---|---|---|---|
| | 16 | 26 | 28 | 34 | 59 |
| Letter | | | | | |
| Value | | | | | |
| Score | | | | | |

## 13. Unhostile Sense of Humor

| Items | | | | | |
|---|---|---|---|---|---|
| | 2 | 6 | 13 | 19 | 29 |
| Letter | | | | | |
| Value | | | | | |
| Score | | | | | |

## 14. Creativeness

| Items | | | | | |
|---|---|---|---|---|---|
| | 8 | 22 | 52 | 57 | 62 |
| Letter | | | | | |
| Value | | | | | |
| Score | | | | | |

## 15. Resistance to Enculturation

| Items | | | | | |
|---|---|---|---|---|---|
| | 20 | 1 | 58 | 69 | 71 |
| Letter | | | | | |
| Value | | | | | |
| Score | | | | | |

## Interpretation

Directions: Enter your total score for each scale in the box provided, and then chart each score at the appropriate point on the graph.

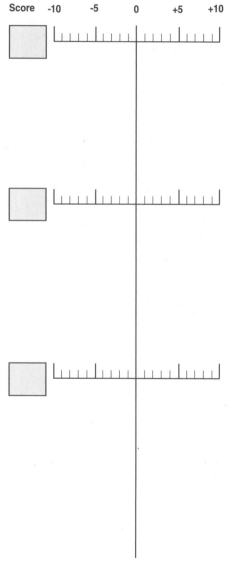

**Scale**

Score  -10    -5    0    +5    +10

### 1. Efficient Reality Perception

Perceiving the real world accurately: making correct discriminations between the real and the spurious; capacity to deal with facts rather than opinions and wishes; appreciation of the unknown as a source for new learning; willingness to let go of the familiar; lack of obsessiveness.

### 2. Acceptance of Self, Others, Human Nature

Acceptance of body and body functions; prizing personal strengths; tolerating inadequacies in self and others; lack of defensiveness; a relative lack of overriding guilt, shame, or anxiety; dislike of pretense in self and others; uncritical understanding view of self and others.

### 3. Spontaneity, Simplicity, Naturalness

Motivated by choice rather than need; in touch with inner feelings and an ability to communicate those feelings effectively to others; an ethical code that is individualized rather than conventional; interest in personal growth and development; appreciation of the simple and unpretentious.

| Scale | Score | -10 | -5 | 0 | +5 | +10 |
|-------|-------|-----|-----|---|-----|-----|

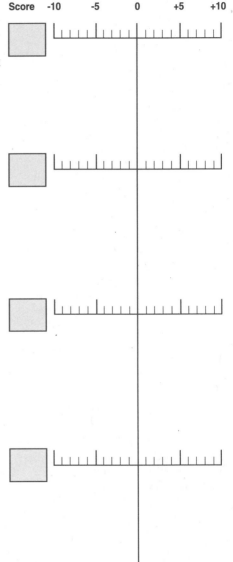

**4. Problem Centeredness**

Ability to focus on problems outside the self; task oriented; lack of self-consciousness; ability to attend to the needs of others; lack of obsessive introspection; concern with basic questions and philosophical issues.

**5. Detachment and Privacy**

Liking solitude and time alone more than the average person; reliance on personal judgments; self-determined; objective; power of focusing and concentration; relationships based on choice rather than need, dependency, or manipulation.

**6. Autonomy and Independence of Culture and Environments**

Indpendent of material things or other opinions; self-motivated; disregard of social rewards or prestige; stability in the face of frustrations and adversity; maintaining an inner serenity.

**7. Freshness of Appreciation**

Capacity for wonder and awe; richness of inner experience; perceiving familiar things as fresh and new; lack of boredom or jadedness; focus on the positive aspects of experience; "original mind"; responsive to beauty.

| Scale | Score | -10 | -5 | 0 | +5 | +10 |

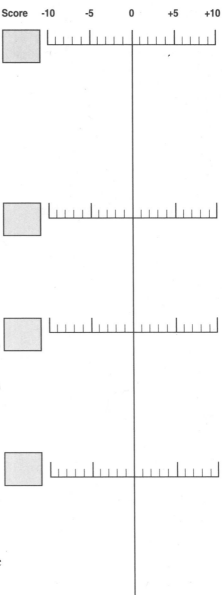

### 8. Capacity for Peak Experiences

Capable of intense, transcendent experiences; ability to experience ecstasy, to move beyond space and time; ability to live in a realm of being and beauty; loss of sense of self, experience of opening up to reality and beyond; capacity to be strengthened and enriched by such experiences.

### 9. *Gemeinschaftsgefuhl*

Feelings of identification sympathy, and affection for all human beings; desire to be of help to mankind; a posture of forgiveness; a belief that humanity is a large family.

### 10. Interpersonal Relations

Capacity for intimacy and closeness; capable of great love for others; benevolence, affection toward many people; choice of a small circle of true, loyal friends; concern for the welfare of others; appropriate anger.

### 11. Democratic Character Structure

Belief in the dignity of all persons; relatively free from biases of class, education, political or religious beliefs, race, or color; focus on character rather than physical aspects of other persons; avoidance of scapegoating; clarity about personal anger and its target.

## Scale

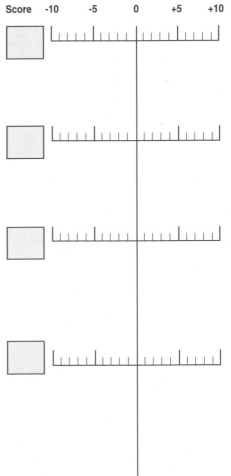

### 12. Ethical Standards

Strong ethical sense, definite moral standards; clear notion of right and wrong; seeking to do right and avoiding wrong-doing; fixed on ends rather than means.

### 13. Unhostile Sense of Humor

Sense of humor devoid of hostility, rebellion, or patronizing manner; capacity to laugh at oneself; appreciation of the ridiculous and the absurd; capacity for playfulness.

### 14. Creativeness

Creativity in everyday life, rather than in artistic endeavors; ability to perceive the true and the real more so than others; creativity that is childlike and playful; having fewer inhibitions or restrictions.

### 15. Resistance to Enculturation

Detachment from the conventional; lack of distortion around authority and authority figures; transcending racial or national distinctions; unconcerned about what is fashionable or chic; ability to live with and to learn from many cultural influences.

Source: Reproduced from The University Associates Instrumentation Kit, "Inventory of Self-Actualizing Characteristics," pages ISAC 4-11. Pfeiffer & Company, San Diego: CA, 1987.

## Choosing a Leisure Pursuit

1. Find your primary interest areas. Check to see the kind of activities that are typical for people with your interests in Appendix 3.
2. In the space provided list your ten favorite leisure time activities in rank order from one to ten. Include activities that you would like to try but have not.
3. The columns that follow ask you to fill in detail about your leisure activities. For example, "Can you do it alone or do you need others?" "Does it cost you money?" "Is it energetic?" "Is it risky in any way?"

| Leisure Activity | Enjoy Alone (A) w/ People (P) | Cost | Emotional (E) Intellectual (I) | Risk: Physical (P) | Active (A), Inactive (I) | Sometimes (S), Rarely (R)? | Done: Often (O) | Last Activity Date |
|---|---|---|---|---|---|---|---|---|
| 1. | | | | | | | | |
| 2. | | | | | | | | |
| 3. | | | | | | | | |
| 4. | | | | | | | | |
| 5. | | | | | | | | |
| 6. | | | | | | | | |
| 7. | | | | | | | | |
| 8. | | | | | | | | |
| 9. | | | | | | | | |
| 10. | | | | | | | | |

What does this say about your leisure life?

Watching television occupies 30 percent of America's spare time, followed by socializing, reading, do-it-yourself projects, and shopping.

Our interests determine how we spend our leisure time as well as the kind of paid work we choose to do. In looking up your most likely leisure activities in Appendix 3 you should find the kinds of things that would appeal to you. However, remember that although many people have leisure interests similar to their paid work interests, some people like their leisure interests to appeal to a different aspect of their personality.

- The results of the interests questionnaire
- The job families that match my interests
- The leisure activities that match my interests

# Rainbow Building Progress Check

## Who Am I?

You have completed your life review, analyzed how you spend your time, identified your work values, discovered your transferable skills, and described your areas of interest. You have also matched your skills and interests against the World of Employment and World of Education maps to see which job families, educational courses, and leisure activities are suited to them.

What have you learned about the types of job that would match your skills and interests?

What have you learned about leisure activities you might pursue?

_____

_____

_____

_____

_____

_____

_____

_____

_____

_____

_____

# Choosing Where to Live

Rainbow Building Skills: Know Yourself, Research Skills

In the past fifty years we have become more mobile than at any time in our history.

American workers will change professions three times and jobs six times over their work lives. Changes will be by choice, at the employee's request, and because new technology restructures jobs or renders them obsolete.

## *Rainbow Builders Always Have a Choice*

This exercise is designed to get you to reassess the choice you have and are making by living where you are now. You can choose to live elsewhere, either at home or abroad. It is increasingly easy to emigrate to other countries, or you may find that your current locale is the right one for you.

- On the next page you will see fourteen clouds displaying twelve different aspects of qualities of living. There are two blank balloons for you to add any aspects important to you but missing from our list. Most of the balloons we think are self-explanatory, but perhaps an explanation of some of them would help you:

  *City/Country* = living in either a city or the country is important to you, or some combination of the two.

  *Proximity to Family* = the distance you live from relatives and in-laws.

  *Cultural Amenities* = availability of theater, cinema, art galleries, schools, stores, restaurants, libraries.

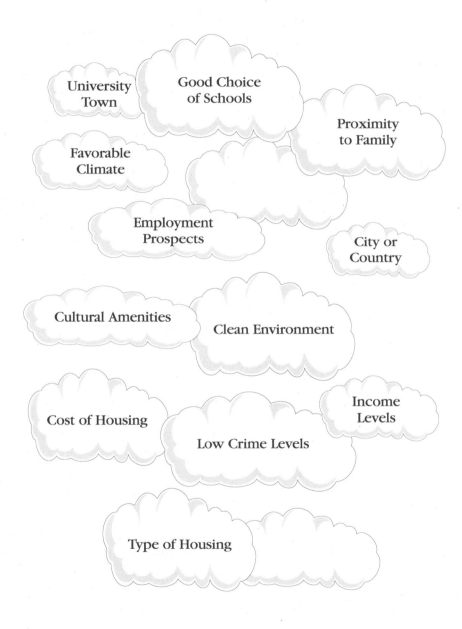

- In the "What I Want From Where I Live" chart, rank order the balloons according to their importance to you. Your most important aspect placed alongside 15, your next most important beside 14, etc.
- Then rate each aspect according to how far that is satisfied by your present place of living by allocating it 0, 1, or 2 in the space provided.

  0 = Not satisfied at all

  1 = Some satisfaction

  2 = Mostly or completely satisfied
- Multiply each ranking by the rating from 0–2, as shown in the example. Then add up the total. This will indicate how well your living needs are being satisfied at present. The maximum total possible is 240, the lowest total possible is 0.
- The following will give you some indication of what your scores mean.

180–240   Well matched. Probably enjoy where you're living. Little reason to look for a change.

140–179   Quite well matched. Some things missing that will need to be compensated for. Not much of an incentive to move.

100–139   Adequate. You often think about moving but probably won't.

60–99   Inadequate. There is much to be desired about where you live. You should seriously be questioning whether you should stay. What in particular are you missing? Is your dissatisfaction widespread or limited to a few items?

0–60   Do you really want to stay???

- You can, of course, use your rankings to compare your present living place with places which you are considering moving to.

- The results of the ranking and rating exercise
- Notes about the quality of life that you would prefer

| What I Want From Where I Live | | |
|---|---|---|
| Quality of Life Aspects | (0, 1, or 2) | |
| | 15 x | = |
| | 14 x | = |
| | 13 x | = |
| | 12 x | = |
| | 11 x | = |
| | 10 x | = |
| | 9 x | = |
| | 8 x | = |
| | 7 x | = |
| | 6 x | = |
| | 5 x | = |
| | 4 x | = |
| | 3 x | = |
| | 2 x | = |
| | 1 x | = |
| | | |
| | Total Points = | |

For example:

| | |
|---|---|
| Favorable Climate | 15 x 0 = 0 |
| City/Country | 14 x 2 = 28 |
| Clean Environment | 13 x 1 = 13 |
| Low Crime Levels | 12 x 1 = 12 |

# Rainbow Building Summary Sheet

## Who Am I?

My major Paid Work Values are

_____
_____
_____
_____
_____
_____
_____
_____
_____

My major Unpaid Work Values are

_____
_____
_____
_____
_____
_____
_____
_____
_____

My major Transferable Skills are in

## People          Data          Ideas          Things

(Circle)

My major Transferable Skills are

_____
_____
_____
_____
_____

I want to live somewhere that has
the following attributes (in order):

_____
_____
_____
_____
_____

# QUESTION 2

# Where Am I Now?

Having identified your skills, values, and interests, and knowing something about your preferred lifestyle, it is now time to stop and examine where you are on your journey through life.

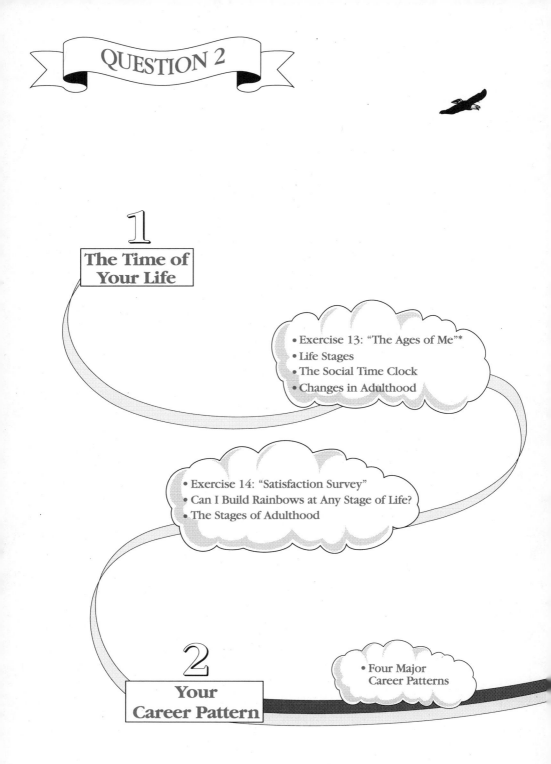

# QUESTION 2

## 1
### The Time of Your Life

- Exercise 13: "The Ages of Me"*
- Life Stages
- The Social Time Clock
- Changes in Adulthood

- Exercise 14: "Satisfaction Survey"
- Can I Build Rainbows at Any Stage of Life?
- The Stages of Adulthood

## 2
### Your Career Pattern

- Four Major Career Patterns

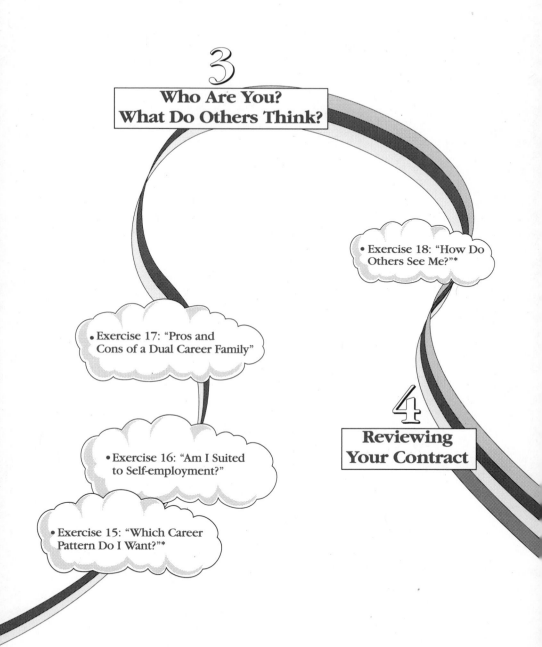

3

## Who Are You?
## What Do Others Think?

• Exercise 18: "How Do Others See Me?"*

• Exercise 17: "Pros and Cons of a Dual Career Family"

4

## Reviewing Your Contract

• Exercise 16: "Am I Suited to Self-employment?"

• Exercise 15: "Which Career Pattern Do I Want?"*

**\* = Essential Exercise**

# The Time of Your Life

## Exercise 13: The Ages of Me*†

Rainbow Building Skill: Know Yourself

Fill in the gaps in the following sentences:

1. In other people's eyes, I look as though I am about _____ years of age.
2. In my own eyes, I judge my body to be like that of a person of about _____ years of age.
3. My thoughts and interests are like those of a person about _____ years of age.
4. My position in society is like that of a person about _____ years of age.
5. Deep down inside, I really feel like a person about _____ years of age.
6. I would honestly prefer to be about _____ years of age.

 What do my answers say about me and how I see myself? What does it say about how I regard aging?

If you are like most people, you will give different ages for the different questions. That is because age is much more than a biological process. It is highly charged with social and emotional significance.

One of the most typical differences in people's answers occurs between the ages they "feel" and their chronological ages. People thirty or over usually "feel" younger than their "official" age. This remains true of many people in their seventies and eighties. It has been found that most people over thirty would prefer to be younger than their actual chronological age. Very rarely, do people actually express a preference for being older, except for some teenagers. The

---

†Adapted with permission of Ayer Company Publishers from Robert Kastenbaum, *Growing Old: The Process of Disengagement.*

fact is that many people do have an aversion to old age, but aging does not have to be a negative experience, and in many cultures is not.

## Life Stages

Modern developmental psychology is notorious for its preoccupation with infancy and adolescence, and its neglect of adulthood. Until recently, if you looked at a typical psychology textbook you would think that human development stopped at age twenty-one. Fortunately writers and philosophers have been more observant, more introspective, and less timid in exploring the longest period of our lives. The Talmud, 2,500 years ago, in the "Sayings of the Fathers," outlined fourteen ages of man, complete with developmental tasks! In 500 BC Confucius identified six steps in the life cycle, while the Greek poet Solon in 700 BC divided life into ten stages, each lasting seven years. More recently and better known, Shakespeare, in *As You Like It,* outlined seven ages of man. But until the 1970s there was almost complete silence from behavioral scientists about the experience of being adult. Daniel Levinson has described the nature of adult life as "one of the best-kept secrets in our society, and probably in human history generally." One of the consequences of this is that people in general have often assumed a stability in adult life that recent research has demonstrated to be the exception rather than the rule. People negate their own experience when they believe it to be unique, thus the myth continues.

Yet along with the concept of stability there is a clear identification in many people's eyes of what is appropriate behavior for one's age. In other words there is an implicit understanding of different stages of life—the experimentation of adolescence, the settling down into a job and marriage, becoming parents and then grandparents, and finally, retirement. The different tasks that accompany these events are talked about, but not so often the psychological changes that occur with them. Consequently, myths develop about the different age groups. Young adults under twenty-five are supposed to be autonomous, exuberant, high in drive to achieve, and reluctant to be "looked after." Therefore, when twenty-five-year-old men and women find themselves apathetic, tired, and depressed by the limited circumstances of their lives, they are doubly depressed—by their actual life situation plus the feeling that people of their age should not be like this. They feel they cannot ask for help from others because they are supposed to be independent. If they enjoy being quiet, low achievers, they suspect that there must be something wrong with them. All too often they jump into roles that they think they "should" be ready for—deciding on a long-term career, getting married, having children—when clearly they are not ready.

Similarly, the myth of the middle years is that adults are responsible, settled, contented, and at the peak of their achievements. But what of those who are not content with their responsibilities and instead wish to explore new experiences and to try new careers or lifestyles?

At sixty to sixty-five years of age, people are supposed to become "old"—ready to retire; lose their health, their wits, and their income; be dependent on their children; be hopeless and unattractive. But what if they are fully fit and alert, fall in love with someone new, want a divorce, or act out a lifelong ambition to travel around the world?

## The Social Time Clock

Bernice Neugarten has suggested that "there exists a socially prescribed timetable for the ordering of major life events" and that most adults conform to this timetable. Remarkable agreement has been found in the general population regarding what age is appropriate for a particular behavior. For example, four in five believe that a man should marry between twenty and twenty-five and a woman between nineteen and twenty-four; that people should finish their education and get a job between twenty and twenty-two; retire between sixty and sixty-five. It is as if there is a social time clock that regulates our lives and by which we judge whether we are "on time" for certain things in our lives.

To be "off time," whether early or late, is to be an age deviant. Like any other kind of deviance, this carries with it social penalties. The woman not married by age twenty-nine used to—and maybe still does—feel embarrassed by it. The man who returns to college at forty-five can feel and be treated as peculiar. It can be as shameful to have a baby at age forty-five as at age fifteen. It does seem that it is harder for a person to go against age expectations in their twenties than in their forties.

The evidence clearly suggests that there are strong culturally transmitted expectations of behavior relating to adulthood. This makes people feel good if they are "on time" and bad if they are "off time." But what is the empirical evidence for some of these age-bound expectations?

## Changes in Adulthood

### Physical Development

The range of individual differences is enormous and no physical change during adulthood can be exactly predicted based on chronological age with the possible exception of grey hair! Longevity and youthfulness run in families and are also more class than age related. People from lower socioeconomic groups tend to age faster, to suffer from poorer health, and to die sooner than those from middle and upper socio-economic groups. Some other findings include the following:

- Maximum height is attained at the beginning of adulthood.
- Physical strength peaks between 25 and 30, after which the muscles—especially in the back and the legs—weaken somewhat unless maintained by exercise.
- Manual dexterity is greatest at about 33.
- Sight diminishes throughout adulthood.
- In middle age, people tend to put on weight around the waist and hips.
- There is gradual hearing loss after 20, especially among men.
- Sensitivity to smell decreases after 40.
- Sensitivity to taste diminishes after 50.
- Appearance alters at middle age—hair greys and recedes, skin coarsens and darkens, wrinkles appear.
- Adults get fewer acute illnesses and more chronic ones than children.
- Older adults take longer to recuperate from illness.
- Sexual potency (quantity not quality!) reaches its peak in late adolescence for men and in the mid-twenties for women.
- Women usually cease menstruation at 40–50.

### Intellectual Development

It used to be thought by psychologists that intelligence followed an inverted U-shaped curve, peaking in the mid-twenties, then declining. However, once the different dimensions of intelligence are examined, the picture looks very different.

- The capacity for rapid processing of information in problem solving ("fluid intelligence") declines steadily from the late teens.

- "Crystallized intelligence," which relates to the storage of information such as vocabulary and general knowledge, increases over the adult years.
- Short-term memory is variable, but long-term memory remains stable, especially with practice.
- Problem solving and reasoning may deteriorate slightly with age, especially when speed is called for.
- Creative output varies widely according to the subject—chemists and mathematicians tend to peak in their twenties and thirties, novelists in their forties and fifties, poets in their twenties, architects in their late forties.

Motivation is obviously a key factor and older people may learn more—and learn it better—because they want more intensely to learn and so work harder at it.

## Exercise 14: Satisfaction Survey

Rainbow Building Skill: Know Yourself

Instructions: On the following list of twenty-five bipolar scales, rate the different concepts: *"Myself Now"* ("M") and *"The Way I Would Most Want to Be"* ("I" for Ideal Self). Place an "M" on each scale in the space that best describes your feeling about that item as it pertains to you *now*. Then go back through the list and place an "I" on each scale in the space that best describes the way you would most want to be in terms of that item. It is possible for your "M" and "I" ratings to be the same.

*Example*

Extremely Somewhat Slightly Neutral Slightly Somewhat Extremely

aggressive: I : M : __ : __ : __ : __ : __ : defensive

In this case, the placement of the "Myself Now" concept on the scale of "aggressive-defensive" indicates that the individual sees himself or herself as "somewhat" aggressive now, but that he or she would like to be "extremely" aggressive.

|                            *Scales*                            | *Points* |
|---------------------------------------------------------------|----------|
| hungry: __ : __ : __ : __ : __ : __ : __ :not hungry          | 1. ____  |
| sexually satisfied: __ : __ : __ : __ : __ : __ : __ :sexually deprived | 2. ____ |
| sleepy: __ : __ : __ : __ : __ : __ : __ :not sleepy          | 3. ____  |
| impotent: __ : __ : __ : __ : __ : __ : __ :energetic         | 4. ____  |
| healthy: __ : __ : __ : __ : __ : __ : __ :sickly             | 5. ____  |
| secure: __ : __ : __ : __ : __ : __ : __ :insecure           | 6. ____  |
| striving: __ : __ : __ : __ : __ : __ : __ :peaceful          | 7. ____  |
| protected: __ : __ : __ : __ : __ : __ : __ :attacked         | 8. ____  |
| in danger: __ : __ : __ : __ : __ : __ : __ :safe             | 9. ____  |
| unopposed: __ : __ : __ : __ : __ : __ : __ :threatened       | 10. ____ |
| not allied: __ : __ : __ : __ : __ : __ : __ :belonging       | 11. ____ |
| with group identification: __ : __ : __ : __ : __ : __ : __ :without identification | 12. ____ |
| accepting of group goals: __ : __ : __ : __ : __ : __ : __ :rejecting of group goals | 13. ____ |
| accepted socially: __ : __ : __ : __ : __ : __ : __ :rejected socially | 14. ____ |
| displaced: __ : __ : __ : __ : __ : __ : __ :having a place   | 15. ____ |
| self-reliant: __ : __ : __ : __ : __ : __ : __ :relying on others | 16. ____ |
| self-respecting: __ : __ : __ : __ : __ : __ : __ :self-disrespecting | 17. ____ |
| self-contemptful: __ : __ : __ : __ : __ : __ : __ :self-esteeming | 18. ____ |
| doubtful: __ : __ : __ : __ : __ : __ : __ :confident        | 19. ____ |
| independent: __ : __ : __ : __ : __ : __ : __ :dependent      | 20. ____ |
| feeling unfulfilled: __ : __ : __ : __ : __ : __ : __ :feeling fulfilled | 21. ____ |
| repetitive: __ : __ : __ : __ : __ : __ : __ :creative        | 22. ____ |
| growing : __ : __ : __ : __ : __ : __ : __ :shrinking         | 23. ____ |
| unadapted: __ : __ : __ : __ : __ : __ : __ :adjusted         | 24. ____ |
| regressing: __ : __ : __ : __ : __ : __ : __ :expanding       | 25. ____ |

## Scoring

1. Count the absolute number of points separating your "I" and "M" marks on each bipolar scale. The difference score is zero if "I" and "M" fall on the same scale point. A maximum score of six is possible on each scale.
2. Write the number of points separating "I" and "M" in the space provided at the right of each bipolar scale.
3. Add the number of points for the first five items and write this score in the space indicated on the following Need Strength Profile grid. This discrepancy score is your dissatisfaction on Maslow's need level I, Basic. Plot this score by placing an "X" on the Need Strength Profile at the correct point for this need. Use the same procedure for each successive group of five items. Thus you will have an "X" on the profile sheet for each of five dimensions representing the five need levels: I (Basic), II (Safety), III (Belonging), IV (Ego-Status), and V (Actualization). Then connect your five "X"s with straight lines to obtain a graphic representation of your need strengths.

*Need Strength Profile*

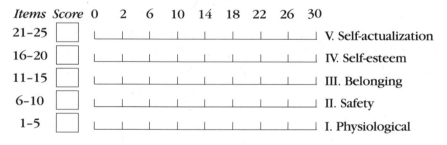

## Interpretation

Your greatest unsatisfied need level is identified by your highest score on the Need Strength Profile grid: your "operating level," then, is the level at which there is the greatest discrepancy between where you are now and where you want to be.

The operating level will dominate your perception. It is most likely that you saw the words in the association exercise through the lens of your operating level. The word "money," for example, may be seen by one person as "paying the rent" but as "shows my status" to another. Pay, then, is not a higher or lower motivator except as it is perceived by the person in relationship to it. "A hero" tends to be seen as a "fool" to someone operating at the safety need level but as "someone to be like" to a person operating at the self-esteem need level. "Independence" is demanded by someone at the self-esteem level and feared by someone at the belonging level. We perceive the world and give it meaning in terms of our own needs.

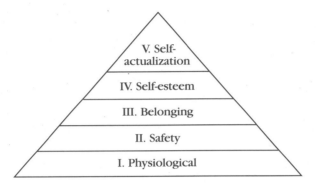

V. *Self-actualization:* inherent well-being, self-fulfillment, personal growth and development, the opportunity to fulfill one's basic potential—to become more like one's natural self

IV. *Self-esteem (Ego-status):* esteem needs for accomplishment, participation, prestige, self-esteem, independent thought and action, privileges, authority, recognition, professional group membership

III. *Belonging:* social needs for affection and caring relationships, trust, feedback, friendships, discussions, being informed, helping other people

II. *Safety:* health care, fringe benefits, routine, stability, financial reward, safety, security

I. *Physiological (Basic):* physiological needs for food, sex, clothing, living quarters, and physical fitness

---

Source: Reproduced from *The 1970 Annual Handbook for Group Facilitators,* Pfeiffer & Company, San Diego, CA.

## Can I Build Rainbows at Any Stage of Life?

Yes, but they will probably look very different at different stages.

The ages presented are indicators only and should not to be strictly interpreted.

| Stages and Tasks of Adulthood | | |
|---|---|---|
| **Stages** | **Ages** | **Task** |
| Pulling Up Roots | 16 | Autonomy, self-sufficiency |
| Provisional Adulthood | 20 | Select career, make relationships, achieve place in society |
| Age 30 Transition | 28 | Search for identity and meaning in life, reassess future objectives |
| Rooting | 32 | Establish long-term goals, get career recognition |
| Midlife Transition | 39 | Reexamine career and personal relationships, assess gap between achievement and aspirations |
| Restabilization and Flowering | 45 | Autonomy, acceptance of time as finite |
| Mellowing and Renewal | 55 — 65+ | Acceptance of what one has, fewer personal relationships, enjoyment of here and now |

## The Stages of Adulthood

Your needs may change depending upon your adult life stage. The following are features of the different life stages.

### Pulling Up Roots (Ages 16–20)

In this stage you seek independence from home and parents or guardians. You ask "Who am I?" "What do I want to be?" "What do I want to do?" You are interested in the values you have inherited and whether they are meaningful as you become independent, explore relationships, test boundaries, and feel your way in a world that is "new" and that you are keen to understand and engage with.

## Provisional Adulthood (Ages 20–28)

During this stage, you are on your own and making your first commitments to work, marriage, family, and other adult responsibilities. During provisional adulthood, you first put to use all of the parental upbringing, education, and advice that were part of your childhood and adolescence. Rarely analyzing commitments, it is time to explore the real world of career, marriage, and lifestyle.

## Age 30 Transition (Ages 28–32)

During this transition stage, initial commitments are often reexamined and their meanings questioned. The surface bravado of the provisional period wavers as life begins to look more complex. You may become impatient with the early choices you made and will feel a new vitality springing from within to answer the question "What do I really want out of life?" Careers and marriages become particularly vulnerable to reassessment. Long-range implications of continuing with current career, community, and lifestyle are challenged. In many people change will occur, and in others there will be a renewed commitment and reaffirmation of their current career, lifestyle, and community.

## Rooting (Ages 32–39)

After going through the Age 30 Transition, there is a tendency to put your head down and get on with life. It is a time when you might seek a mentor—a patron or supporter to show you the ropes. Then at about age 35, the time-squeeze begins. Perhaps it is the first emotional awareness that death will come and that time is running out. Now you want more than ever to become established. When you start a career or family, you launch them with certain goals and dreams. Some of these are attainable and desirable and others are not. This time-squeeze during the rooting process often is a cause of concern. "Is there still time to change?"

## Midlife Transition (Ages 39–45)

Also known as midcareer or midlife crisis, this is often a period of acute personal discomfort in which you may face the gap between youthful dreams and actual fulfillments. Likely limits of success and achievement become more apparent. There may be a gap between what you have reached and what you want. For some people, this transition is merely a decade milestone. For others, it can be a painful time of crisis. Children are growing up and going away, and for many their parents are now looking to them for support. You ask many self-searching questions in this period, such as "What's in it for me?" "Where am I having fun?" "Why can't I be accepted for what I am, not what 'they' (spouse, boss, society) expect me to be?" "Is there one last chance to make it big?" In the search for answers that often consumes the midlife transition period, you may seek a new career or other new directions in life.

### Restabiliztion and Flowering (Ages 45-55)

Once we have gone through the midlife transition, faced mortality, and forged a new lifestyle, this stage can feel like the best time of life. Unrushed by comparison to the urgency of the thirties, a new stability can be achieved. A career often takes a sharp turn upward. Money becomes less important. Life can become more stable because you listen more to the inner voice than to external demands. You may experience increasing attention to a few old values and a few friends. One hypothesis is that in this and the next stage, if we lose a spouse or close friend, we may go back into Provisional Adulthood patterns, trying out life options all over again.

### Mellowing and Renewal (Ages 55-65+)

At this stage, you tend to be more satisfied with yourself, coming to grips with what you have and haven't done. At first, there is little concern with either past or future, but eventually questions arise as to when to retire, what to do, and how to cope with sudden changes in lifestyle. It is a difficult step because nearly all of our life is attuned to paid work. Thus, an abrupt shift to leisure is sometimes traumatic. The impact of this decision can be compounded by aging, termination of longtime associations and friendships, and, frequently, by a total lack of preparation.

Be wary of theories that tell you what you should be doing, thinking, or feeling at any particular life stage. Life is not as neat as that. You can be largely restabilizing and flowering but also be dealing with some leftover midlife transition issues, or even some rooting.

The value of research like this is not to create new psychological and behavioral strait jackets, but to let you know that the changes and complexity you might be experiencing are not being experienced in isolation. But although the process is valid enough in general, there will be considerable individual differences.

Likewise, the process described now belongs to this historical epoch. It would be rash to presume that fifty years from now, within a different society with new concepts of work, leisure, and the family, that the stages would remain as they are described here.

Gail Sheehy, in her book *Pathfinders,* did a nationwide survey of reported satisfaction from men and women that produced some fascinating differences. From their late twenties women get increasingly dissatisfied with life and only catch up again with men in their early fifties. Her research also suggests that women take longer to resolve their midlife transitions than men. The period between forty and fifty-five represents the time when the sexes are furthest apart in terms of life satisfactions. Women only became happier than men at the end of their lives (presumably after many of the men have died!).

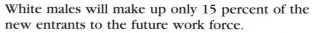

White males will make up only 15 percent of the new entrants to the future work force.

Women-owned business is one of the fastest-growing segments of the U.S. economy.

Marcel Proust in his book *Remembrance of Things Past* noted that every one of us

> ...is a creature without any fixed age who has...the faculty of becoming, in a few seconds, many years younger, and who, surrounded by the walls of time through which he has lived, floats within them but as though in a basin the surface level of which is constantly changing, so as to bring him into the range now of one epoch, now of another.

Daniel Levinson expanding on this theme says that

> Only after we understand the profound significance of the epochs in our lives...can we understand the ways in which one is, at a single time, a child, a youth, a middle-aged, and an elderly person. We are never ageless. As we gain a greater sense of our

own biographies, however, we can begin to exist at multiple ages. In the process we do not fragment ourselves, rather we become more integrated and whole.

 About 45 million of today's full-time workers are not covered by private pension plans.

- Your Scores from the Satisfaction Survey
- Notes about what you learned from the Stages and Tasks of Adulthood table and how these descriptions compare with your actual age and feelings

 Do I recognize myself?

The following cartoons represent some of the most common life stage problems. The important thing to remember is that all of these problems are normal. That does not mean that your uniqueness is in any way reduced, but it might help to see yourself in perspective. All of these people are desperately in need of rainbows. By working through this book they could all create opportunities for themselves to build some.

## *A Gallery of Life Stage Problems*

*Sarah Secretary*—34 years old

"I really could do an administrative or supervisory job—couldn't I?"

"I do seem to have as many skills as a lot of my so-called bosses."

"My boss keeps pushing me to be more ambitious."

"Is it worth it when I would have to move if and when my husband moves?"

"My husband wouldn't mind as long as it doesn't affect him or the children."

*Peter Plateau*—45 years old

"Why am I always being passed over?"

"Why doesn't my boss give me challenging assignments?"

"Just what do you have to do to get promoted around here?"

"Why can't my wife and I communicate better?"

"Why do my children seem to believe in everything I don't?"

*Cathy Catchthirty*—30 years old

"I know I'm doing well, but something seems missing."

"Why am I so depressed?"

"I really would like a baby—wouldn't I?"

"I don't really want a baby—do I?"

"Why can't I be satisfied with what I've got? Most women in my situation would be really happy."

*Terry Technician*—26 years old

"This really seems as far as I can go with my present qualifications."

"Do I want to be an engineer with all that would be involved?"

"If I do all that studying it will really take up a lot of my social life and domestic time. Will it all be worth it?"

"Can I be certain that there will be a good job for me at the end of it all?"

*Michael Mellowed*—53 years old

"I've spent a good part of my life doing this. I've done it well and I've done well—but there's no challenge any more. It's all too easy."

"What else can I do at my age?"

"Can I really spend another twelve years just doing the same thing?"

"Could I afford to make a change? My kids have left home, but we are used to a good standard of living."

# Rainbow Building Progress Check

## Where Am I Now?

 What did I learn from the Satisfaction Survey?

What did I learn about my life stage problems? Do I have any?

_____

_____

_____

_____

_____

_____

_____

_____

_____

_____

_____

_____

_____

_____

_____

_____

# Your Career Pattern

Just as the concept of work is changing dramatically, so is our concept of career. Traditionally the word career has come to mean a succession of jobs each of which has higher status and income than its predecessor. People who did not progress in this way were sometimes referred to as merely having "jobs," while those who did progress had "careers." We can now recognize that it makes more sense to distinguish between a variety of career patterns.

## Four Major Career Patterns

Following the work of Michael Driver, we identify four major career patterns from which people tend to choose. The Career Patterns diagram describes the four patterns, states at what life stages this choice tends to be made, the frequency of occupational changes that the people (given the choice) would make, and the directions of the career pattern viewed in hierarchial terms. It also summarizes the motives behind the choice of pattern. The following people are examples of the different patterns.

### Horizontal—John (40)

"I've never had a job for more than two years. I get bored. I don't always leave for more money. Sometimes I've earned less. But I like learning new things, meeting new people—it's interesting. I don't suppose I'll ever change now. Some people think my jobs are "dead-end jobs," but I reckon some of those folks who spend all their lives working their way up are half dead by the time they get there."

### Steady—Carol (30)

"I've always wanted to be a nurse. Even before I went to school I had a nurse's uniform. It would be nice to get to be a registered nurse. I'd hate to be a supervisor—all that paperwork and responsibility, and you don't have the same relationships with your patients. I'll do this until they kick me out."

### Vertical—Charles (55)

"I always wanted a good job with prospects. I've always been ambitious, and I've done well. I had to swap firms a bit during my thirties and forties but each one moved me up a rung or two. I like the responsibility now. I like making decisions."

### Cyclical—Janette (49)

"I really like to get involved in what I'm doing, but I do like learning new things. I made a vow to myself in my twenties that no matter how well I was doing, every five years or so I'd take a good hard look and see if it was still exciting me. If not, I'd change. I've changed occupations three times now and don't regret one of them. I hope to do at least two more very different jobs before I die."

## Exercise 15: Which Career Pattern Do I Want?*

Rainbow Building Skill: Know Yourself

Look at the Career Patterns table and then answer these questions.

 Which career pattern is closest to the one I've had?

Circle your choice.

     Horizontal      Steady      Vertical      Cyclical

 Which is the closest to the one I would like in the future?

Circle your choice.

     Horizontal      Steady      Vertical      Cyclical

| Career Patterns | | | | |
|---|---|---|---|---|
| **Type of Career** | **When Choice of Pattern Is Made** | **How Often Occupations Are Changed** | **Direction of Change** | **Motive for Choosing This Pattern** |
| Horizontal "Variety" | Never. People do not consciously make a choice. | 1–2 years | Levels are not relevant | Variety, challenge, "doing what you want to do, regardless" |
| Steady "More of the same" | Teenage choice | Never or rarely unless forced | Stays the same | Security, intrinsic job satisfaction, wanting "a job for life" |
| Vertical "The ladder" | Teenage choice | Never or rarely unless forced; jobs are changed for advancement | Upward | Achievement, status, material success, power |
| Cyclical "The 5-year itch" | Every 5 to 10 years | 5–10 years | Levels are not relevant | Variety, personal growth |

There are many other decisions to be made about career patterns prior to the one represented by the options of the four major types in the diagram. You will be asked to think some more about this.

## *Decision 1. Do I want to work full-time or part-time?*

Part-time work is increasing rapidly. It has been affected less than full-time employment by the recession and the shift from an Industrial to a Post-Industrial Economy.

To some extent this is misleading. What is changing is our concept of employment. People are beginning to ask themselves for how many hours they wish to perform paid work each week, or even, in a year. The average work week is reducing, albeit slowly. You can anticipate a future where people will do paid work from a few hours to fifty hours a week for a few weeks to almost every week of the year, for a number of years to a full lifetime.

  A record 7.2 million people have more than one job. That's 6.2 percent of all workers.

### Decision 2. Will I be employed by someone else or will I work for myself?

The fastest growing area of the economy is self-employment. There has been almost a thirty percent increase in the past ten years. The enormous growth of the "black economy" also demonstrates how many people like to work for themselves.

The majority of new jobs are being created in small business. We can no longer look to large companies to provide the nation with new jobs. To expand and develop they have to shed labor not increase it.

  Two out of three new businesses fail by the end of five years.

## Exercise 16. Am I Suited to Self-employment?

Rainbow Building Skill: Know Yourself

Here are some arguments for and against self-employment. Put a check in the box if you are attracted by what it says. The total number of checks in each section is your score for that section.

### A. By being self-employed...

☐   1. I would be my own boss.
☐   2. I could work when I wanted to and stop when I felt like it.
☐   3. I could use my own money to do something useful.
☐   4. I would be free and independent.

☐ 5. I would learn about business.

☐ 6. I would improve my self-confidence.

☐ 7. I would be able to work day and night at something I like doing.

☐ 8. I would avoid being unemployed and all the problems that go with it.

☐ 9. I would welcome the chance to think up an idea for a business.

☐ 10. I would have to make plans.

☐ 11. I would have to organize my time carefully.

☐ 12. I would be able to make money out of an idea I've got.

☐ 13. I could make a lot of money.

☐ 14. It would give me experiences that I could use later in life.

☐ 15. I could look for other jobs while working as a self-employed person.

Total checks _____

## B. By being self-employed...

☐ 1. I would have to work on my own a lot.

☐ 2. I might have to spend all my savings.

☐ 3. I would have to start working early every morning.

☐ 4. I would probably have to work in the evenings.

☐ 5. I would have to organize myself and my work very carefully.

☐ 6. I would have to persuade other people to help me.

☐ 7. I would have to sell things or ideas to strangers.

☐ 8. I would have to find premises or run the business away from home.

☐ 9. I would have to give up a wage or benefit that I could receive each week.

☐ 10. I may have to borrow money from family or the bank.

☐ 11. I may have to give up a regular job.

☐ 12. I may have to go to an evening class to learn business skills.

☐ 13. I would have to find out if there's any kind of need or demand for my skill or product.

☐ 14. I would have to find out how to keep business records.

☐ 15. I would have to work very hard.

Total checks _____

| Self-employment Evaluation | | |
|---|---|---|
| Section | Score | Meaning |
| A | 11–15 | You are clearly the type to be attracted by the idea of working on your own account. |
| | 8–10 | You are drawn to the idea, but should find out more about it. |
| | 0–7 | You are the cautious type. |
| B | 11–15 | You are prepared to pursue the idea, even though you see how difficult it could be. |
| | 6–10 | You are interested but still anxious. |
| | 0–5 | You'd be better off in a regular job. |
| Total Score (A+B) | 20–30 | Self-employment could well be the route for you. |

If you try these tests again in a year's time, you could score very differently.

## Decision 3. Am I or will I be part of a dual-career family?

We believe strongly in the value of a couple doing this program together. This is essential if both partners have jobs. Couples are beginning to discover that having a dual-career family can offer greater opportunities for each individual than if either was the sole breadwinner. It makes sense to decide what income is required as a family and then examine the various alternatives. This can then enable both partners to share more in parenting if they wish or to develop other interests and unpaid work skills that possessing a full-time job would inhibit. Real life examples have included:

- Both partners taking part-time jobs
- One partner taking a year off to do other things
- One partner decreasing his/her job to seventy-five percent to provide time for other activities.

The following figure shows a wide spectrum of career relationships possible within the context of a marriage.

## A Spectrum of Relationships for Couples

| Traditional* Couple | Semi-Traditional Couple | Typical Dual-Career Couple | Egalitarian Couple |
|---|---|---|---|
| He is the breadwinner. | He is the bread-winner (with some involve-ment in family and home). | He is committed to a professional career. | His and her roles vis-a-vis career and home are essentially the same. |
| She is the home-maker and child-raiser. | She is the home-maker and child-raiser but she also works, usually for a narrowly defined purpose (such as better vacations for the family, extra home comforts, her own personal satisfaction). | She is committed to a professional career. | Both work; they have an equal commitment to their jobs. |
| He provides financial security. | He has the domi-nant career but acknowledges her contribution to their quality of life and her need for some kind of outside activity. | The couple think of themselves as being a dual-career family. | Both do fifty percent of the housework. |
| She provides child care and social maintenance. | She works, but neither of them thinks of her as having a "career." | But, one of them (almost always the woman) takes on more than fifty percent of the responsibility for housekeeping and child-raising, and one provides sub-stantially less than fifty percent of the income. | Both do fifty percent of the child-raising. |

Notes: *Traditional as used here may still be relevant for some; however, it was a more appropriate description for couples from the late 1940s through the early 1970s.)

Couples often change their relationships on the spectrum. Perhaps the most typical example we see of this today is the couple who in their twenties assume a traditional couple role. In their thirties, after their children are in school, they shift to the semi-traditional role. And in their forties, after the children have left home, they become a dual career couple. In practice, however, at this stage, women typically are a number of years behind men who have had full-time, uninterrupted careers.

Where on the spectrum am I and my partner?

We should not always take for granted what people mean when they say that they are a "dual-career family." The majority of such couples may have dual careers, but they may not have an egalitarian relationship when it comes to domestic responsibilities.

 Women now head 29 percent of U.S. households.

## Exercise 17: Pros and Cons of a Dual-Career Family

Rainbow Building Skills: Know Yourself, Make Decisions

- Each partner makes a list of
  A. The advantages of being part of a dual-career family.
  B. The disadvantages of being part of a dual-career family.
- Share the lists and discuss.

 Overall, do we wish to be a dual-career family?

What are the implications for us of being a dual-career family?

*Decision 4. What career pattern do I want?*

This has already been examined. The decision-making process that you need to follow is summarized in the following diagram.

| | Decision 1 | Decision 2 | Decision 3 | Decision 4 |
|---|---|---|---|---|
| **?** | | | | Horizontal "Variety" |
| | Full-time | Self-employed | Dual-Career System | Steady "More of the Same" |
| | Part-time | Employed | | Vertical "The Ladders" |
| | | | | Cyclical "5-Year Itch" |

My notes on options and careers to consider.

Assuming an annual inflation rate of 5 percent, a worker making a $50,000 salary would need to increase it to $81,445 within 10 years just to maintain buying power.

# Rainbow Building Progress Check

## Where Am I?

 What have you learned about the possibilities for your own career pattern?

_____

_____

_____

_____

_____

_____

_____

_____

_____

_____

_____

_____

_____

_____

_____

_____

## Who Are You? What Do Others Think?

Up until now you have been involved primarily in collecting data from yourself only on who and where you are. The final part of Question 2 will involve you getting data from other important people in your life. To see yourself as others see you is a vital element in rainbow building. Don't allow yourself to be shaped by other people, but be open to the possibility of learning from others.

The Johari Window is a useful way of looking at oneself, and it demonstrates the different facets that contribute to that unique individual—Me!

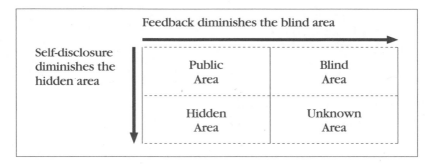

*Johari Window*

### Public Area

This refers to those personal aspects that you know about and that you are comfortable for others to know about too.

### Blind Area

Those parts of ourselves that others see but of which we remain in blissful ignorance. This has been called the "bad breath area," but this only refers to negative aspects of ourselves. Often you are unaware of positive or interesting things that people think and feel about you because they have never told you and you have never asked them.

## Hidden Area

Your innermost thoughts and feelings, expressed to few or perhaps to no one.

## Unknown Area

This is sometimes called the area of potential growth. It refers to the potential you possess that has not yet come to light.

You need to get feedback from others to discover more of your blind and unknown areas.

### Exercise 18: How Do Others See Me?*

Rainbow Building Skills: Know Yourself, Research Skills, Communicate

This exercise involves a process that you might wish to initiate to a greater or lesser extent.

You should have completed exercises on the following:

1. My lifeline
2. How do I spend my time?
3. My work and play values
4. Finding my transferable skills
5. What are my interests?
6. Choosing where to live
7. The ages of me
8. What stage am I at now?
9. What kind of career pattern do I want?

You will undoubtedly obtain value from talking through your answers to these, and any of the other exercises, with friends and colleagues, but there are particular exercises where additional data can be invaluable. Here are some suggestions.

- Get a spouse or close friend to do the Work Values card sort in terms of the values they see you demonstrating. From this you will learn which values they see you expressing as well as merely holding.
- Ask friends and colleagues to do the Transferable Skills card sort according to how they see your skills.

- Ask colleagues and your bosses what skills they see you as owning. Ask them also what areas for development they see in you.
- Ask a spouse or friend to do the Interests check according to what interests they see you as having.

In addition to these you might like to ask your spouse or partner to do the exercises on where they would like to live and work.

- The results of the exercises about me completed by other people
- Notes about aspects of myself which have been revealed

# Rainbow Building Summary Sheet

## Where Am I Now?

| I am at the following life stages | The career patterns I want: (circle) |
|---|---|
| _____ _____ _____ | Horizontal  Steady  Vertical  Cyclical<br>Dual Career<br>Full-time            Part-time<br>Employed            Self-employed |

I have learned the following about myself from other people:

_____

_____

_____

_____

On the basis of that I will

_____

_____

_____

_____

You are now about midway through this career and life management program. You have collected a great deal of data about yourself. Reflect on the following and record your thoughts for your Aha! folder.

How do I feel about myself and who and where I am right now?

What changes would I like to make?

# Reviewing Your Contract

Now will be a good time to refer back to the contract you made with yourself. Look back to what you have written and write in your answers to the questions below.

What have I got so far from working with this book?

_____

_____

What have I been doing to get what I want?

_____

_____

Have I been sabotaging my efforts in any way?

_____

_____

How am I feeling about building my rainbows right now?

_____

_____

What else must I do to maximize my chances of getting what I want?

_____

_____

Am I committed to continuing with the process?

_____

_____

## QUESTION 3

# How Satisfied Am I?

Having thought about "who you are" in terms of your career and life so far, the next step is to reflect on the amount of satisfaction and dissatisfaction you are currently experiencing. Satisfactions can be clues to what is important to you and what you may want to preserve and retain. Dissatisfactions, on the other hand, are clues to what in your career or life may need remedying. This is not to say that you can achieve everything you desire, which is clearly not the case, as constraints—both internal and external—must limit everybody's range of choice. Frequently, however, we limit our thinking by focusing so directly on the constraints operating on us that we are able to achieve less than we might. In consequence, our careers or lives may not be as consciously shaped, chosen, or satisfying as they might be.

The exercises in this section will help you to focus, in turn, on

- Your sources of satisfaction.
- What you would like more, or less, of in either your present job, your career, or your life.
- Objectives you may wish to set in order to achieve more of what you feel is important to you.

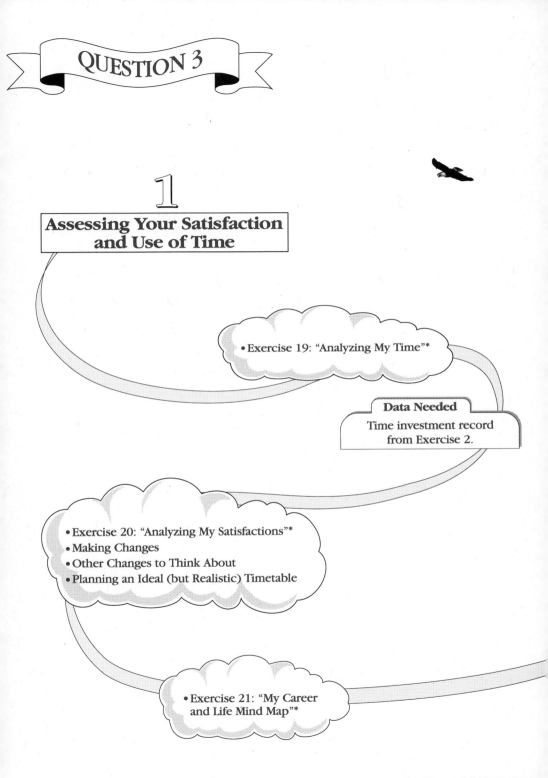

QUESTION 3

1

**Assessing Your Satisfaction
and Use of Time**

• Exercise 19: "Analyzing My Time"*

**Data Needed**

Time investment record
from Exercise 2.

• Exercise 20: "Analyzing My Satisfactions"*
• Making Changes
• Other Changes to Think About
• Planning an Ideal (but Realistic) Timetable

• Exercise 21: "My Career
and Life Mind Map"*

**\* = Essential Exercise**

# Assessing Your Satisfaction and Use of Time

In Section 1, Exercise 2, you completed a Time Investment Record and asked yourself questions about this. Now is the time to assess the level of satisfaction you are getting from that investment when compared with the time spent. It is useful to distinguish between Maintenance, Sold, and Discretionary time.

- Maintenance Time—Time spent maintaining yourself or others, cleaning, eating, shopping, cooking, sleeping, etc. Keeping things moving along in your life.

- Sold Time—The time you "sell" to an employer, an organization, or a customer, to produce income or some other reward. This concept is wider than simply the hours you spend "doing" your job. It involves time spent traveling to work, follow-up time, etc.

- Discretionary Time—Free time that you choose exactly how you want to use. This may not always mean that you will enjoy what you choose to do. You may feel a responsibility to attend a local committee meeting, to visit relatives, or to learn a new skill, but you might not particularly enjoy any of these activities. It is your choice, however. It may not always feel like you have a choice, but you do.

There are always alternatives. You may choose an action because you don't want to face the consequences of an alternative, for example, facing criticism from others or dealing with your own feelings of guilt. But for every situation there are alternatives.

Sometimes the distinctions between these three elements of your time can be difficult to make. Everyday cooking is clearly a maintenance activity. If it is also a hobby of yours, you may spend much longer at it than you need to. In that case you are devoting some of your discretionary time to cooking too. These distinctions have to be subjective. Only you can decide under which of the three labels a particular activity comes.

## Exercise 19: Analyzing My Time*

Rainbow Building Skills: Learn From Experience, Know Yourself

## Analyzing Your Time

- Use three differently colored pencils to color in each section according to whether it is maintenance, sold, or discretionary time.
- Now work through the Time Investment Record and list your activities under each of the three categories using labels that make sense to you. Your lists might look something like the following:

| *Maintenance Time* | *Sold Time* | *Discretionary Time* |
|---|---|---|
| Sleeping | At work | Time with my spouse |
| Eating | Traveling to work | Walking |
| Cleaning | Work at home | |
| Shopping | | |

- Take a large sheet of paper. Write your lists on the left-hand side and mark off two-hour time segments across the top to make a chart like the one in the following Time Analysis Example. Try to get as many time divisions as possible across your sheet because "sleeping" and "at work" each could take up to sixty hours.
- Looking back at your Time Investment Record, add up as accurately as possible the total time spent on each activity over the whole week. Using the same colors as before, mark off the bars on the chart to show the total. When you have finished, check how much of the bars you have colored in; it should represent close to 168 hours (the hours available to you in one week).

### Time Analysis Example

| *Maintenance Time* | 2 | 4 | 6 | 8 | 10 | 12 | 14 | 16 | 18 | 20 |
|---|---|---|---|---|---|---|---|---|---|---|
| Sleeping | | | | | | | | | | |
| Eating | | | | | | | | | | |
| Cleaning | | | | | | | | | | |
| Shopping | | | | | | | | | | |
| *Sold Time* | | | | | | | | | | |
| At work | | | | | | | | | | |
| Traveling to work | | | | | | | | | | |
| Work at home | | | | | | | | | | |
| *Discretionary Time* | | | | | | | | | | |
| With spouse | | | | | | | | | | |
| Walking | | | | | | | | | | |

Beware of too broad categories. In the example, "At work" should be broken down further and, similarly, discretionary time "with spouse" should be broken down into what was done and for how long.

## Exercise 20: Analyzing My Satisfactions*

Rainbow Building Skills: Learn From Experience, Know Yourself

Work down your list again and assess how much satisfaction each activity gives you using the star system below. Record your star rating next to each activity on your chart.

| | |
|---|---|
| ✳ | Very Unsatisfying |
| ✳✳ | Somewhat Unsatisfying |
| ✳✳✳ | Somewhat Satisfying |
| ✳✳✳✳ | Satisfying |
| ✳✳✳✳✳ | Extremely Satisfying |

How does your chart look? Are your highly rated activities the ones you are spending plenty of time on? Are there any shocks?

## Making Changes

It's worth thinking about the activities you might like to do more of. Not all activities that are relatively satisfying give more satisfaction if you do a lot more of them—they may be better in small doses.

Look at each of the activities to which you have given a four- or five-star rating. Think about which ones really would give you extra satisfaction if you could do more of them. Some will be easier to increase than others.

If you do want to do more of some activities, where will you find the time? You will have to reduce the time spent on some other activities. Which ones will you choose and how will you spread the cutbacks? Not all activities with a low rating will be easy to cut, but start by looking at low-rated activities in your "Discretionary" group.

Are there any activities that are missing altogether from your busy life you would like to include?

## Other Changes to Think About

Look back at your notes about the balance of your life roles (see Exercise 2) and see if they suggest any other changes you might want to make.

Were any of the roles missing from your life?

Do you want to change the balance of time spent in different roles?

## Planning an Ideal (but Realistic) Timetable

You may have decided you would like to increase or decrease the amount of time spent on some activities, or you may have decided that increases are unnecessary but that protection of certain time is important. Start with types of activity you wish to increase or protect and make a set of decision statements like the one below.

I plan to spend at least four hours per week exercising.

- Your bar charts for time and satisfaction
- Your ideal time chart

## Exercise 21: My Career and Life Mind Map*

Rainbow Building Skill: Know Yourself

This exercise is designed to take a snapshot of your entire life as you experience it now. This will help you to draw up a list of your primary satisfiers and dissatisfiers. A technique that many people find helpful in getting many related and unrelated thoughts on to paper in a short period of time is called mind mapping. The example below may, at first glance, look totally chaotic, but closer inspection will reveal the thinking "flows" that occurred when the person produced this mind map.

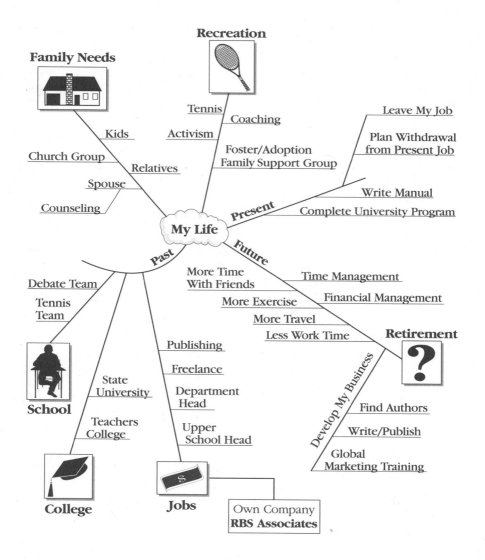

The advantages of mind maps over ordinary list making are

- The main idea is clearly defined.
- The relative importance of each idea is clearly indicated—more important ideas will be nearer the center and less important nearer the edge.
- New information is easily added.
- Links between ideas are easier to see.

The mind map example will give you an idea of the process. You always begin a mind map in the center of a large piece of paper with the key concept, in this case "My life." See what comes into your head. Don't worry about order or presentation as this will interrupt your thinking flow. Put everything you can think of around the central idea. After you have finished, see what links to what and connect them. You can always redraw your pattern if it will make it easier to understand. Use different colors to distinguish between your primary branches, either by writing with different colors or by circling the branches with different colors.

1. Print your main idea in the center of the paper enclosed in a shape.
2. Branch out from the center. Name the branch lines close to the center, for example, "Past, " "Present," "Future," etc. Take it as far as your mind wants to take it.
3. Create branches to hold the important points or ideas, adding details or key words to the main branches.
4. Use symbols and images along with words.
5. Print neatly so the pattern will be easier to read later.
6. The printed words should be on lines and each line connected to other lines.
7. Use one color for conditions, aspects, and ideas in your mind map that denote "satisfiers." Circle any item that seems to be a "satisfier" for you.

List all your satisfiers on a separate sheet of paper. Each time one is mentioned, write it down, for example:

| | |
|---|---|
| family | travel |
| job | community activities |
| friends | learning/studying |

- On the same sheet of paper write down the answers to the following questions using the appropriate words from your list:

Who are the key people in my life and career?
What do I need from my paid or unpaid work?
What do I enjoy doing? What surprised me?
Is there anything missing?
Would I have expected some satisfiers to be here which are not? Why aren't they on my mind map?
Which of my satisfiers would I like more of?

- Now circle all the items on your mind map that are "dissatisfiers" in some way. Use another color for this. You might even find that some items classify both as satisfiers and dissatisfiers.
- List all your dissatisfiers on a separate sheet of paper as you did for the list of satisfiers.
- Write down your answers to the following questions:

Who are the key people in my dissatisfactions?
What do I need from my paid or unpaid work?
What don't I enjoy doing? What surprised me?
Is there anything missing?
Which of my dissatisfiers do I want to do something about?

- Your mind map
- Lists of satisfiers and dissatisfiers

Over 73% of men over 65 are retired from the labor force.

According to Peter Drucker, over 90 million people work as volunteers either full- or part-time.

# Rainbow Building Summary Sheet

## How Satisfied Am I?

You have analyzed in greater depth just what payoffs you are getting from how you spend your time. You have delved into what really gives you satisfaction in your career and your life and explored the causes of your dissatisfaction. It may be useful to summarize these under the headings of People and Activities. However, if you have items that do not really fit this classification, create another more appropriate one.

| *My Major Satisfiers Are* | | |
|---|---|---|
| In My Job | People | Activities |
| In My Career | People | Activities |
| In My Life | People | Activities |

| *My Major Dissatisfiers Are* | | |
|---|---|---|
| In My Job | People | Activities |
| In My Career | People | Activities |
| In My Life | People | Activities |

## QUESTION 4

# What Changes Do I Want?

Not everybody can attain or achieve absolutely everything; however, most of us rarely achieve all that we are capable of, largely because we are not clear about what we want or would prefer. Until we are, we cannot even begin the journey toward our next stage of development through which we will realize more of our potential and achieve more of what is important to us.

QUESTION 4

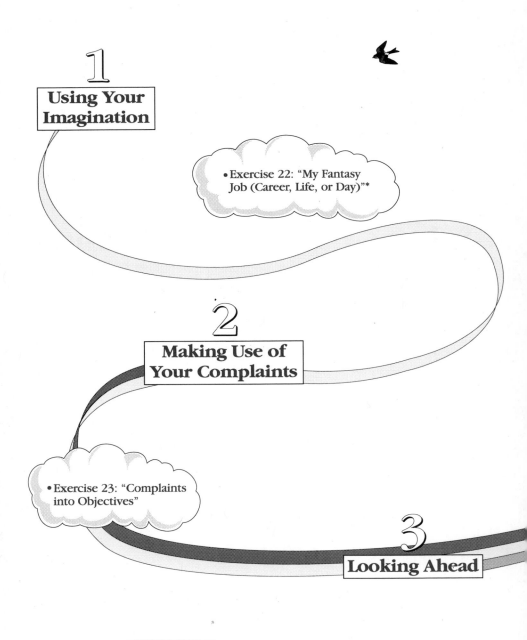

1
**Using Your Imagination**

• Exercise 22: "My Fantasy Job (Career, Life, or Day)"*

2
**Making Use of Your Complaints**

• Exercise 23: "Complaints into Objectives"

3
**Looking Ahead**

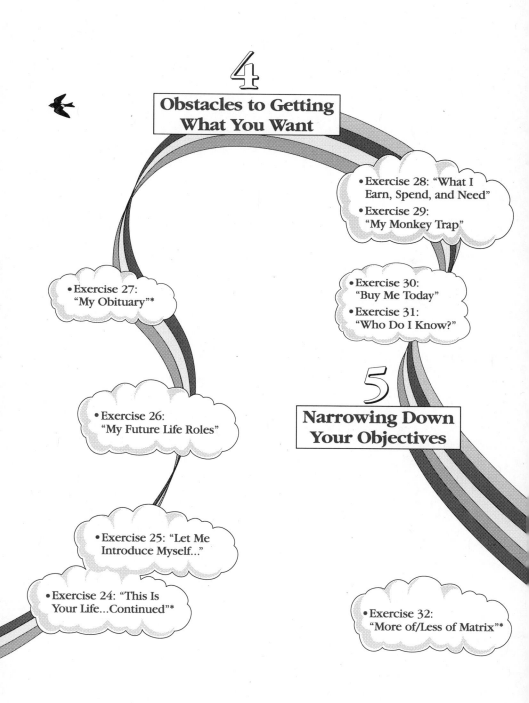

# 4
## Obstacles to Getting What You Want

- Exercise 28: "What I Earn, Spend, and Need"
- Exercise 29: "My Monkey Trap"

- Exercise 27: "My Obituary"*

- Exercise 30: "Buy Me Today"
- Exercise 31: "Who Do I Know?"

- Exercise 26: "My Future Life Roles"

# 5
## Narrowing Down Your Objectives

- Exercise 25: "Let Me Introduce Myself..."

- Exercise 24: "This Is Your Life...Continued"*

- Exercise 32: "More of/Less of Matrix"*

**\* = Essential Exercise**

# Using Your Imagination

The first exercise in this section invites you to use what for many is an underused dimension—your imagination. In your hard, practical, workaday world this speculative, potentially creative faculty is often regarded as largely escapist and detached from reality, and therefore of doubtful value. Those who spend too much time using their imagination are often labeled "dreamers," which implies an element of time wasting and is regarded largely as pointless. We challenge this.

In using your imagination, or in a fantasy journey, what you can do is to get in touch with those possibilities that would be interesting, attractive, or desirable for you. Such flights of fancy can provide clues as to where you would like to be or what you might want to work toward—which, because it seems too impractical, you may have scarcely even bothered to think about. Using your imagination, thinking the unthinkable, dreaming the impossible, need not be a waste of time.

This kind of exercise will be easier for some personality styles than for others. The practical, logical person might respond less enthusiastically, inclining toward hard, researched, proven data and methods. The enthusiastic individual often takes more readily to the possibility. Whatever your inclination, however, there are gains to be made from an excursion into the realm of fantasy. Give it a try!

## Exercise 22: My Fantasy Job (Career, Life, or Day)*

Rainbow Building Skill: Know Yourself

- Imagine for a time that there are no constraints on you for time, money, age, experience, health, status, ties, etc. Remove all thoughts of constraints for the next few minutes—ignore them!
- Appreciating that there are no restrictions, select one of the following to work on. Begin with whichever seems easiest and circle it:

|  |  |
|---|---|
| My Fantasy Job | My Fantasy Day |
| My Fantasy Career | My Fantasy Life |

- Think through your chosen topic in some detail and write down your version of what would be involved. For example, in your Fantasy Job identify details such as status, salary, job specification, style of work, the accompanying lifestyle, what you would actually do and not do, with whom you would work, in what kind of surroundings, authority and responsibilities involved, and typical workday or week.

In your Fantasy Career examine your career as a whole, commenting, for example, on how it might ideally develop from your present position. Include your preferences and wants in such areas as career progression, status, income, employment pattern, desired lifestyle, opportunities for using your present skills and developing others, integration of your career development with other life roles, and opportunities you hope will occur for you.

Your Fantasy Day is an invitation to log the events of what for you would be the "perfect day." Where would you be, what would you do, and with whom, if anybody? What time would the day start and end? Would it include work, leisure, or family and in what proportion?

Your Fantasy Life offers an opportunity to consider your ideal life as a whole. In this fantasy you can outline what would be your scenario for the perfect life. This picture could include how long you would like to live, your work pattern, home and social life, status, income, and lifestyle.

Whichever topic you choose, write in as much detail as you can so that the fantasy becomes a full picture rather than simply an outline. If you prefer to represent the details of your fantasy in picture form or through symbols rather than in written words, please do so. The more details you have, the more useful the exercise will be to you.

- When you have written down your fantasy, it is ready to be worked on. Think carefully through the following:

What are my thoughts, feelings, and reactions to doing the exercise? What does the fantasy indicate about what I would value, appreciate, aspire to, or want for myself?

What are the differences between my fantasy and my reality? How much of my fantasy is achievable at present or might be in the future? If I can't have it all, can I have some of it?

What are the barriers to my achieving some of my fantasy and how might these be overcome? What would be the consequences of my working to achieve some of the features of my fantasy, for myself and for other people?

Would the pursuit of the features of my fantasy and their achievements be worth the possible consequences? What objectives would I like to set for myself on the basis of this exercise?

Make a note of any objectives you have identified and place these in your "Aha!" folder.

- Your fantasy
- Things you need to achieve your fantasy

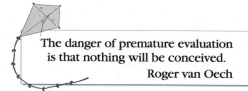

The danger of premature evaluation is that nothing will be conceived.

Roger van Oech

You see things as they are: and you ask, "Why?" But I dream things that never were: and I ask, "Why not?"

George Bernard Shaw

# Making Use of Your Complaints

## Exercise 23: Complaints Into Objectives

Rainbow Building Skill: Learn From Experience

Sometimes it is easier to focus on what you do not like in a particular situation than on what you do like. Irritants and dissatisfactions are often easy to identify because of the discomfort they cause; it is difficult to ignore things which actually hurt. But remember, pain alerts us to something that needs attention.

Your complaints and dissatisfactions can therefore be used positively. They bring to your attention something you would prefer to be different, and they form the starting points from which to make changes—so that things will be more like you want them to be.

By being explicit about what you don't like you can discover more of what you do like. Complaints can be converted into objectives!

This exercise invites you to look at current complaints you may have about your job, career, or life and to use them to begin to identify what you might work to change.

### Complaints

Sometimes dissatisfactions are expressed in very general terms ("I am not getting much out of my job at the moment") and this means they are difficult to translate into objectives. To help make your complaints specific, look at your job in more detail. If you choose to look at your life, your career, or just one day, you will probably need to add your own categories. But, just for this example, our focus is on features of your job that commonly provide sources of dissatisfaction—if for you there are other sources, then simply add them to the "Job" column.

- In the "Complaints" column of the chart, briefly note any significant complaint you may have in a particular area. Consider each area in turn. For example, for People/Relationships you might record "not enough contact with colleagues."
- Enter not applicable (N/A) for areas about which you have no complaints.

## Examples

- In this column, note a specific example of your complaint. The more specific you can be, the more you will know what needs to be tackled. For example, for People/Relationships you might write "No coffee break—we each take coffee in our own office."
- When you are through, ask yourself:

How do I react to seeing what I have written? How great/small, typical/rare are my complaints?

How much are the matters I complain about my responsibility? Others? Are there complaints for which I can't provide examples?

## Objectives

The next step is to translate complaints into objectives. Your complaints are comments on "how things are" at present. Begin to describe "how you would like things to be."

- Take each complaint in turn and write in the objective column what you would like to do to improve things. Continuing with our example for People/Relationships where the complaint is "Not enough contact with colleagues" your objective might be "To organize social area for coffee breaks."
- Try to express each objective in positive terms. Refer to what it is that you want to do—setting objectives for somebody else can be very ineffective!
- Be specific and set a definite time by which you hope to achieve your objective. Objectives stand more chance of becoming realities if you act positively, take responsibility, and know specifically what you wish to achieve and by when.

## Success Indicators

In the last column, try to list the result of achieving your objective—whatever will be the mark of success for you. Identification of a specific example can be a check of how realistic your objectives are—if the example looks very remote and unlikely, you may want to review your objectives.

It is particularly useful to talk through your plans for turning complaints into objectives with another person. That can be really helpful, since it will

- Encourage you to explore and clarify your dissatisfactions and what you will do about them.
- Offer the possibility of a "contract for change" in which you openly declare your intentions (and are more likely, therefore, to be committed to achieving them).
- Invite support for some of the things you wish to do.

| Complaints Into Objectives | | | | |
|---|---|---|---|---|
| Job | Complaints | Examples of Complaints | Objectives | Success Indicators |
| People/ Relationships | | | | |
| Finances | | | | |
| Prospects | | | | |
| Activities or tasks | | | | |
| Time | | | | |
| Surroundings | | | | |
| Life style | | | | |
| | | | | |
| | | | | |

Source: Adapted from Loughary and Ripley

Place any objectives you have as a result of this exercise in your "Aha!" folder.

- Your completed worksheet
- Any objectives you came up with

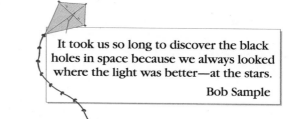

It took us so long to discover the black holes in space because we always looked where the light was better—at the stars.

Bob Sample

No one ever stumbled across anything sitting down.

Charles Kettering

## Rainbow Building Progress Check

### What Changes Do I Want?

The last two exercises have provided a way of thinking about changes you would like.

What have I learned about what I would like to change?

_____

_____

_____

_____

_____

_____

_____

_____

_____

_____

_____

_____

_____

_____

# Looking Ahead

## Exercise 24: This Is Your Life...Continued*

Rainbow Building Skill: Make Decisions

Return to your completed Exercise 1: "Drawing My Lifeline." Continue your lifeline adding as many details as you can for your future life. Then reflect on these questions:

Is my desired lifeline very different from how I think my life will continue? What might prevent me from getting the lifeline I want? What can I do to get more of what matters to me?

- Your new lifeline
- Notes

## Exercise 25: Let Me Introduce Myself...

Rainbow Building Skill: Communicate

This is a verbal variation of the last exercise.

- Find a colleague with whom you can do this exercise.
- Take ten minutes to introduce yourself as you are now.
- Next, spend five to ten minutes introducing yourself as the person you were exactly ten years ago. This is more powerful if you speak in the first person—as if it really was you but ten years younger.
- Finally, spend five to ten minutes introducing yourself as the person you think you are most likely to be ten years from now. Again, try to keep it in the first person.

Which introduction was most difficult? Why?

Is there a difference between what I hope my life will be like and what I realistically think it will be like ten years from now? What are the implications of this for my future decision making?

Notes describing your vision of your future life

## Exercise 26: My Future Life Roles

Rainbow Building Skill: Make Decisions

In Section 1 you completed a Time Analysis Record showing what proportion of time you spend in your range of life roles.

- Imagine yourself ten years from now. Write down what you would see yourself being and doing for each life role.

| Future Time Analysis Record | | | | | | | |
|---|---|---|---|---|---|---|---|
| *Percentage of Time Spent* | | | | | | | |
| Life Role | 10 | 20 | 30 | 40 | 50 | 60 | 70–100 |
| Child | | | | | | | |
| Employee | | | | | | | |
| Spouse | | | | | | | |
| Parent | | | | | | | |
| Citizen | | | | | | | |
| Consumer | | | | | | | |
| Friend | | | | | | | |
| Pleasure seeker | | | | | | | |
| Student | | | | | | | |
| Homemaker | | | | | | | |
| | | | | | | | |

The completed list

## Exercise 27: My Obituary*

Rainbow Building Skills: Know Yourself, Learn From Experience.

Obituaries include an evaluation of a person's life and describe the person's life history, achievements, and key relationships.

- Write your obituary as an objective journalist might, including the time and manner of your death. Limit it to six hundred words. Although you may experience difficulty or distress in doing this exercise, it is of great value. Upon completion of your obituary, consider these questions:

How would I summarize that person's life? Can I think of a fitting epitaph? Write it here.

How might I have liked that obituary to read differently? What can I do now to ensure that my obituary will read the way I want it to?

_____

_____

_____

_____

_____

_____

_____

_____

## Rainbow Building Progress Check

### What Changes Do I Want?

  What have I learned about the sort of future I
would like for myself?

_____

_____

_____

_____

_____

_____

_____

_____

_____

_____

_____

_____

_____

_____

_____

_____

_____

# Obstacles to Getting What You Want

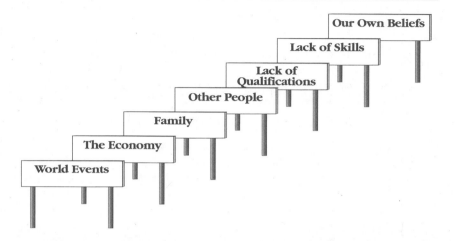

The hurdles are designed to prevent us from getting what we want. Some are outside of our control—World Events and the Economy; some are partially under our control—Family, Other People, Lack of Qualifications and Skills; one is totally under our control—Our Own Beliefs. Let's examine some of the beliefs that we have found to be blocks to rainbow building.

### *"If I have problems, it means I'm inadequate."*

It is normal to have problems. Life is about progressing from boring problems to fascinating ones. Instead of thinking of it as a "problem," see it instead as a discrepancy between what one has and what one wants. Then turn the complaint into an objective.

### *"It's better to keep my problems and thoughts to myself."*

Not if you want to build rainbows! There are genuine personality differences to consider. Some people like to talk things through with others, while some prefer to work through an issue by themselves. Research findings indicate that problem solving is almost always improved by involving other people. There may be times when we need to be alone to sort things out, but any conclusions or decisions will undoubtedly benefit from discussion with people who you know are useful resources and providers of feedback.

*"I cannot live on less than I earn now."*

In our experience this is hardly ever the case. What is required is a careful identification of present income and expenditure matched alongside priorities. Test this out for yourself with Exercise 28.

## Exercise 28: What I Earn, Spend, and Need

Rainbow Building Skill: Set Objectives, Make Action Plans

- Prepare a budget sheet for you or your family. A typical budget sheet is reproduced here, but don't think you must use this one as it stands. It may not fit for you. Feel free to design your own. Additional predesigned budget planners and worksheets are available from any store that sells office supplies.

| Budget Sheet | | | | |
|---|---|---|---|---|
| Income | Amount | Expenses | | Amount |
| Salary/Wages | | Money | Savings | |
| | | | Finance charges | |
| | | | Rent/mortgage | |
| Interest | | | Rates | |
| Perks (company car, bonus) | | | Insurance | |
| | | Auto/Travel | Loan payment | |
| | | | Taxes | |
| Other | | | Insurance | |
| | | | Fares | |
| | | | Gas | |
| | | | Service, repairs | |
| | | Food | Groceries | |
| | | | Meals out (incl. school) | |

| | | Budget Sheet (continued) | | |
|---|---|---|---|---|
| Income | Amount | Expenses | | Amount |
| | | Vacations | Travel | |
| | | | Lodging | |
| | | | Other | |
| | | Household expenses | Utilities | |
| | | | Fees (trash, sewage) | |
| | | | Phone | |
| | | | Cleaning | |
| | | | Yard/Landscaping | |
| | | | Other | |
| | | Enter-tainment and leisure | Newspapers/Magazines | |
| | | | Shows/Movies | |
| | | | Sports | |
| | | | Hobbies | |
| | | | Lessons | |
| | | | Other | |
| | | Clothing | Clothes, shoes | |
| | | | Dry cleaning | |
| | | | Repair | |
| | | Miscellaneous | Birthdays | |
| | | | Holidays | |
| | | | Hairdresser | |
| | | | Other | |
| Total Amount | | Total Amount | | |

Begin by determining what you absolutely must have to live, as opposed to what you would like to have. For example, could you sell your car and travel by bike or bus? Could you sell your existing house for a profit and buy a cheaper one if you are financially strapped? You may need a vacation but can you find a home-exchange plan instead of a hotel?

Before you say "Well, that takes all the fun out of life!" remember, that we are looking here at what is absolutely necessary.

 What have I eliminated? Can I gain the satisfactions provided by those items elsewhere or in a cheaper way?

For example, you could limit dinners out and experiment with a new cuisine at home or buy fewer books and use the public library more.

 If I were starting up again just what would I need? (Strip away the present accoutrements and expectations you have developed over the years.) Do I really still need all the income that I have? What are the implications of this?

One conclusion might be confirmation of insufficient income. Your issue would then be to generate some alternatives to acquire extra income. (See Resources Section)

 Your budget sheet and analysis

You may trap yourself into a lifestyle because of assumptions of what you need to make life worthwhile. Your desires can sometimes be so consuming that you pursue goals that clearly are not in your own best interests.

In some parts of the world where people enjoy monkey meat, they have developed a novel way of trapping monkeys. A coconut is hollowed out through a small hole in the shell. Boiled rice, which monkeys apparently adore, is placed inside the hole, which is just big enough for an average-sized monkey fist to squeeze through. The shell is tied to a tree. Now, when the greedy monkey discovers the shell and the rice, he also discovers that he can just get his hand inside the shell, but as soon as he takes a handful of rice, he cannot get his hand out again! The monkey, you might predict would drop the rice to escape. But instead he cannot bring himself to let go and sits watching the hunters come closer and closer until they club him to death.

Most of us have our own monkey traps—things, ideas, or people— that we cannot let go of even if it means our stagnating and perhaps even dying, psychologically and even physically (e.g., stress-related diseases). We must have material possessions, or job security, or the permanence of a relationship at all costs, or a belief of how the world should be as opposed to how it is. Looked at this way, perhaps it is easier to understand just how a monkey can be so stupid!

## Exercise 29: My Monkey Trap

Rainbow Building Skill: Know Yourself

Think about the story of the monkey trap and write down an equivalent trap in your life.

What is my "rice"? What could I gain if I let go of my rice? Are there any different kinds of rice?

Is the trap the only place where I can find rice? Is there more than one kind of rice? Is the rice really worth risking my life? What is holding on to the rice costing me?

*"It is undignified to have to promote or sell oneself."*

This relates to a huge myth, namely, that talents will always be spotted. Experience suggests that talents first have to be demonstrated. Why should anyone have confidence in you unless you give them some evidence for it? Exercise 30 will invite you to do this. Of course, you cannot provide that evidence unless you have it. That is why your answers to *Question 1: Who Am I?* are so crucial.

*"Somewhere in the world there is the job waiting for me."*

From Question 1 you should have discovered that for your interests, skills, and values there will be many jobs that you could do and would probably be very happy doing. To a large extent, too, a job is what you can make of it. Jobs are not like ready-to-wear clothes that you have to fit yourself into. While there will always be limits to the pattern, to a certain extent you can always cut some of your own cloth.

*"The job I have now is ideal and therefore it always will be."*

We have already discussed the rapid rate of technological change, which means that in the unlikely event that you stay exactly the same, the chances that your job will stay the same (or even remain) are minimal.

Just as new needs develop and old needs are satisfied for our lives in general, the same is true about jobs. A research study (Campbell, D.) has shown that a person's needs from a job change over time. To begin with, job security and safety is vital—ensuring that you are seen as competent enough to hold the job. Next comes the need to be accepted and to have one's work recognized. During these stages, too much autonomy and challenge may actually prevent you from performing at your best. These factors assume greater importance only after your more basic needs are met.

The same research showed that after fifteen years or so, even the most enriching job tends to become boring. The message is that you must periodically review what you are getting out of your job and that you should not get angry with yourself or worry if you become dissatisfied with what you have previously found satisfying. That is what life is about. It is called *development.*

*"Whatever I do or plan is useless. It will all eventually be determined by...my firm...my family...the government."*

There will always be factors out of your control, but many things are open to your influence. In the final analysis you always have control over your own reactions to an event or decision. You can create unnecessary frustration by assuming that you can or should be able to influence everything. You cannot change the world but you might be able to change your bit of it.

*"Somewhere in the world there is the personnel manager, the firm, or the boss who will discover me and my potential."*

How? Not unless you make yourself known, communicate your skills and qualities, and market yourself as a desirable product. If you can't be bothered to advertise yourself, why should anyone else be interested enough to do it for you?

## Exercise 30: Buy Me Today

Rainbow Building Skill: Know Yourself

- Imagine yourself to be a product. Your task is to launch this new product successfully. To sell any product successfully, you need to believe in it. To believe in it you need to know what it is capable of along with any deficiencies or problems there might be because you, as the salesperson, will be held accountable.

We have reproduced an example of a completed Personal Product Analysis. We would like you to produce

A. A product analysis of your assets,

B. A product analysis of your problem areas,

C. An assessment of your development needs,

D. An appropriate sales slogan, if you were to promote yourself as a "product," and

E. A rationale for why someone should buy a "product" like you.

## Personal Product Analysis Example

| A. Summary of Assets | B. Summary of Problem Areas |
|---|---|
| *Skills* <br> Can drive, type, organize, write, research, communicate well | *Skills* <br> Tends to over organize vs. produce, poor number skills |
| *Personal Qualities* <br> Enthusiastic <br> Determined <br> Conscientious | *Personal Qualities* <br> Easily distracted <br> Can be over jolly |
| *Values* <br> Reliable <br> Honest <br> Hard working | *Values* <br> Needs to be appreciated <br> A bit "goody-goody" |
| *Other* <br> Willing to share skills <br> Looks younger than age | *Other* <br> Tendency to flare up <br> Doesn't bother about appearance |

**C.** What further development is required for this product?

This product needs better packaging and more drive to do really well. It is rather conventional and ordinary at the moment but could be marketed as a fun package for special occasions.

**D.** Create a sales slogan that typifies this product and simultaneously presents it in a favorable light.

Will work cheerfully to achieve any job undertaken.

**E.** In fifty words or less say why you would buy this product.

I would buy this because I need an energetic and hard-working person who will be a reliable addition to a team. I value honesty and reliability and find that people with these qualities are valuable as supporters and organizers. Most importantly, the "can-do" attitude of this product is very appealing.

| *Personal Product Analysis* | |
|---|---|
| **A. Summary of Assets** | **B. Summary of Problem Areas** |
| *Skills* | *Skills* |
| *Personal Qualities* | *Personal Qualities* |
| *Values* | *Values* |
| *Other* | *Other* |

**C.** What further development is required for this product?

**D.** Create a sales slogan that typifies this product and simultaneously presents it in a favorable light.

**E.** In fifty words or less say why you would buy this product.

I would buy this because

*"It's unethical to think of people in terms of how helpful they might be to my career."*

Using people as resources is not the same as "using" people in some manipulative way, especially if we are also open to be used as resources by others. People are invaluable for information, for support and sometimes for advice. Armed with specific questions you can learn more about a job or a leisure pursuit in 30–60 minutes from a well-informed person than from spending 6 hours in a library. One of the most valuable things you can do in searching out job opportunities and leisure options is to "plug" yourself into networks or people. We so often fail to ask for help from the human resources that are all around us and at our disposal.

Most new jobs are filled as a result of people hearing about them from friends or as a result of a direct approach to an employer.

- Your "product analysis"
- An advertisement for yourself

## Exercise 31: Who Do I Know?

Rainbow Building Skill: Research Skills

List the names of relatives, friends, and colleagues on a piece of paper. Check your address book. These need not be people who are immediately obvious as useful contacts and their purpose may only become apparent later. You will probably find that you have at least one hundred names already. This is your Personal Contact Network.

Yet each of these people has a Personal Contact Network of their own, which gives you access to from five to ten thousand people even allowing for overlap between networks.

- Begin to analyze your own network.
- What jobs are represented?

- What interests?
- What skills?
- What special knowledge?

Your network

## Narrowing Down Your Objectives

### Exercise 32: More of/Less of Matrix*

Rainbow Building Skill: Set Objectives

This matrix is useful for consolidating all of the possible areas for personal change that the rainbow building process has identified thus far. If you find that it inhibits you rather than facilitates you, don't use it. You will need to find an alternative way of collecting your personal data to enable you to decide which areas of your life require some action.

- Using the following Matrix, in each category identify what you would like more of, or less of, in terms of contact with particular people or in terms of the activities you spend time on. (The central column, "Keep the Same," can be used to register what is satisfactory at present; you may find it useful to enter details in that section also.) The more specific you can be in your entries, the more useful they are likely to be at the next stage. Produce your own matrix on a large sheet of paper if this one is not large enough.

When you have filled in the form, circle the three things that you would most like to do something about right now.

| More of/Less of Matrix Example | | More of | Keep the Same | Less of |
|---|---|---|---|---|
| Present Job | People | *Contact with colleagues doing similar work* | *The amount of contact time with clients (as distinct from staff)* | *Staff seeking approval for decisions they have already taken* |
| | Activities | *Creative planning sessions for new ideas* | *Amount of responsibility and supervision of others' work* | *Routine paperwork* |

| More of/Less of Matrix | | More of | Keep the Same | Less of |
|---|---|---|---|---|
| Your Present Job | People | | | |
| | Activities | | | |
| Your Career | People | | | |
| | Activities | | | |
| Your Life in General | People | | | |
| | Activities | | | |

# Rainbow Building Summary Sheet

## What Changes Do I Want?

What have I learned from my fantasies about what changes I want in my life?

_____

_____

_____

From my life review and my life choices exercises I know that I want to change...

_____

_____

_____

What objectives do I have arising from my complaints?

_____

_____

_____

What stops me from getting what I want?

_____

_____

_____

Do I want to do anything about it, and if so, what?

_____

_____

_____

What is my personal advertising slogan?

_____

_____

_____

What three things do I want more of?

_____

_____

_____

What three things do I want less of?

_____

_____

_____

# How Do I Make
# Them Happen?

The key to getting more of what you want, to making things more like you want them to be, is likely to be the precision with which you can set objectives and make action plans. Failure to achieve much of what we would like in life can be traced to one or all of the following:

- Low motivation
- Unclear objectives
- Ill-formed action plans

We are assuming that, like all rainbow builders, you will be motivated to work for what you want, so we would now like you to give attention to clarifying your objectives and identifying the steps you will take to achieve them.

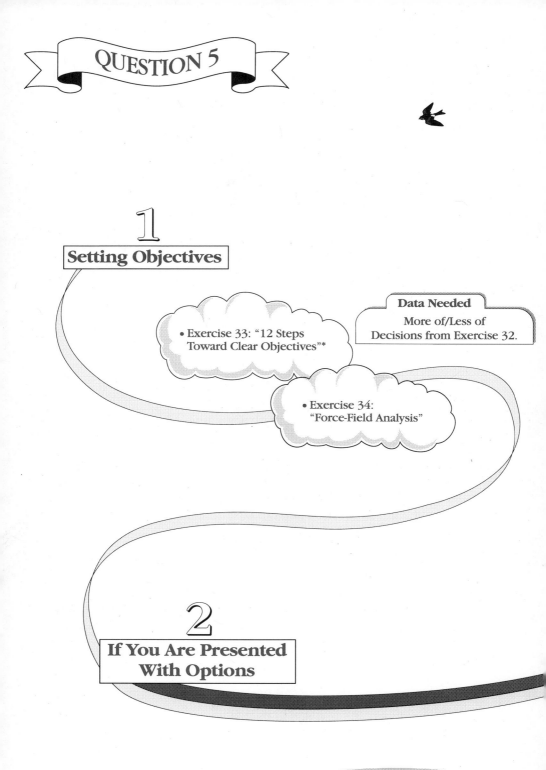

QUESTION 5

1
**Setting Objectives**

• Exercise 33: "12 Steps
Toward Clear Objectives"*

**Data Needed**
More of/Less of
Decisions from Exercise 32.

• Exercise 34:
"Force-Field Analysis"

2
**If You Are Presented
With Options**

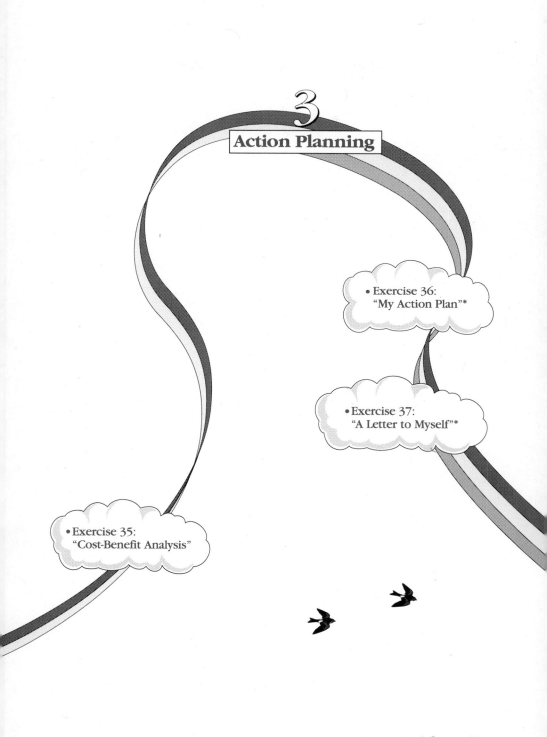

# 3
## Action Planning

• Exercise 36:
"My Action Plan"*

•Exercise 37:
"A Letter to Myself"*

•Exercise 35:
"Cost-Benefit Analysis"

* = Essential Exercise

# Setting Objectives

An objective is a desired outcome, target, or result. It states what you want to achieve. For example, "I want to get a job that involves less stress and gives me more free time."

Objectives are important in defining what we want, in giving us a sense of direction, and in offering us a chance to shape our own development. Remember "If you don't know where you are going, you will probably end up somewhere else!"

An objective states simply what we want to achieve, it does not describe tasks or activities that we will undertake to achieve it—those will be part of your action plan to achieve your objectives. For example, "I will buy a selection of newspapers to look for job vacancies" is part of an action plan.

## Exercise 33: 12 Steps Toward Clear Objectives*

Rainbow Building Skills: Set Objectives, Make Action Plans, Make Decisions

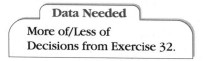

**Data Needed**
More of/Less of
Decisions from Exercise 32.

- Write down on separate pieces of paper each of the three objectives you wish to do something about.
- For each objective, take the following steps. Write down your answers. At the end of this process you should have defined at least three clear objectives.

1. State your objective clearly. Start with the word "To..." followed by an action word. For example, "To work for promotion to head of department in my present job."
2. Ask yourself whether there is an objective behind your objective. Ask why you want what you want—there may be other

ways of getting it; for example, if you are pursuing responsibility, status, or extra money there may be other ways of achieving it without actually being promoted.

3. State clearly how you will know when your objective has been reached; this will ensure that your objective is clear.

4. Make your objective as specific as possible, for example, not "I want my life to be more rewarding" but, "I want to get more satisfaction from my job by replacing some of the paperwork with time to do creative planning."

5. State when you want to achieve this by and why you choose that date. For example, "I want to achieve promotion by this time next year, because to wait longer would be frustrating."

6. Be clear for whom you want this. If it is not for yourself, will the other person find the objective desirable, or even acceptable?

7. Check whether any of your objectives conflict. For example, if you have said that you want to work for promotion to department head but also that you want to spend more time with your family, then you have to decide whether these two objectives are compatible. If any of your objectives conflict, then you will obviously have to identify which ones have priority and work on those.

8. Identify any constraints (external or internal) that will make your objective more difficult to achieve.

9. Identify any resources (external or internal) that will assist in the achievement of your objective.

10. Check that your objective is realistic. As before, talking it through with someone else or with several other people can provide useful alternative perspectives on how to tackle it.

11. Ask whether there is anything to stop you achieving your objective now. If not, you are ready to start. But if there are obstacles, then obviously your initial objective is to work to overcome those particular constraints.

12. How do you feel about what you have just decided to do? You may need someone who will give you real support while you work on achieving your objective.

The process can be repeated for any number of objectives.

State your three objectives

## Exercise 34: Force-Field Analysis

Rainbow Building Skills: Set Objectives, Make Action Plans, Make Decisions

Force-field analysis is a way of improving your chances of achieving an objective or an action plan. It can be a method for examining what is involved in changes we may be thinking of making and of identifying which forces may be helpful in making the changes and which may work against the changes. The method was developed by Kurt Lewin to demonstrate efficient and inefficient ways of achieving personal change.

In any situation where we wish to make a change there will always be some forces assisting us and some forces resisting us.

Consider the following example:

> Emma and Bill live in New York. They both have good, well-paying jobs. They have always talked of moving to the country, away from the city and nearer to Emma's parents who are getting older. Bill is not happy in his present job and has found a business close to where her parents live which he wants them to take on together. Emma, however, has excellent career prospects and does not want to give them up now. How then does Bill attempt to create conditions that will render Emma more open to change? A typical approach is to extol the virtues of the new scheme: the chance to live in the country, to get away from the rat race of the city, and to be near enough to her parents to visit more often. However, using this approach is more likely to increase resistance to any move than to inspire Emma to join him.

The following diagram represents the forces working for and against Emma's acceptance of this move.

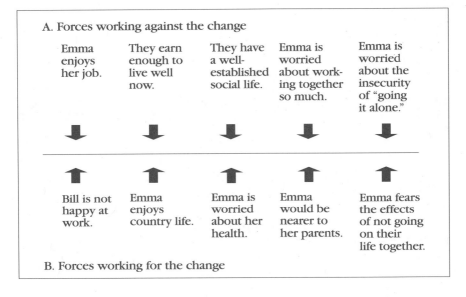

A. Forces working against the change

| Emma enjoys her job. | They earn enough to live well now. | They have a well-established social life. | Emma is worried about working together so much. | Emma is worried about the insecurity of "going it alone." |

| Bill is not happy at work. | Emma enjoys country life. | Emma is worried about her health. | Emma would be nearer to her parents. | Emma fears the effects of not going on their life together. |

B. Forces working for the change

The approaches that Bill has tried have all been concerned with reinforcing the upward pressures, namely emphasizing the beneficial effects a move could have for him, for their lifestyle, and for her parents.

However, our model is something of a physical one, and every physicist knows that if the forces operating on an object in a state of equilibrium are increased in one direction, then the forces in the opposite direction must increase equally if the equilibrium is to be maintained. This means that our arrows now look like this:

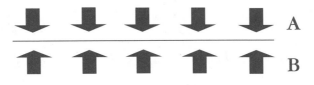

What happened is that forces operating on each side are now significantly stronger, and tension is at a higher level. Emma's frustration will increase, and her resistance is likely to harden.

What happens if Bill uses the other alternative open to him and concentrates on the downward forces (A) that make Emma resistant to change? This approach is called reducing resistance. If Bill tackles her concerns about the scheme and succeeds in reducing her resistance, then a new equilibrium is reached, but at a lower level of tension. This is like stopping a car by taking one's foot off the accelerator, without using the brake.

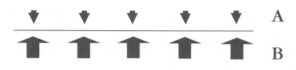

The following exercise invites you to use this approach, alongside the more traditional one of building on the forces working for change.

The technique is to:

1. Identify your objective.

   - State what you want to achieve, very specifically using the word "To..." and including when you hope to achieve it ("...by...").
   - Make sure you have stated only one objective. Deal with them one at a time!

2. List the forces working in favor of what you want to achieve

   - A positive force is anything that will contribute to your achieving your objective.
   - When listing forces, be very specific (what, who, where, when, how much, how many). Remember these forces may be inside or outside of you.
   - Indicate how the force will help you to achieve what you want.

3. List all the forces working against what you want to achieve.

   ■ Again, be specific.

   ■ List all factors, inside or outside yourself that will work against you.

   ■ Indicate what effect each force is likely to have on your achieving your objective.

4. Analyze the forces.

   ■ Identify which forces are most important. These forces should be real, not assumed, and will have a significant effect on whether or not you can achieve your objective.

   ■ Circle all the important forces on your list.

   ■ Obtain any additional information you feel you may lack about any important force.

5. Weaken the negative—strengthen the positive.

   ■ Work on each important force in turn.

   ■ Identify ways in which you can reduce, minimize, or eliminate (not exterminate!) each force working against you. Indicate any that you really cannot find a way of reducing by writing "no action possible" against it.

   ■ Identify ways in which you can increase, strengthen, or maximize each positive force. Work on one at a time.

6. Assess how feasible your objective or action plan seems to be.

   Ask yourself: Do the positives clearly outweigh the negatives or will they when I have maximized and minimized them?

   ■ If the answer is "yes," ask yourself again "Do I really want to achieve this?"

   ■ If the answer again is "yes," adopt your objective and begin to work on these forces.

   ■ If the answer is "no" for either question, then your choice is to abandon it or change it. For example, if may be possible to modify the original by reducing your sights or revising the target time.

# If You Are Presented With Options

## Exercise 35: Cost-Benefit Analysis

Rainbow Building Skills: Know Yourself, Make Decisions

It can be useful in choosing from among different options to see the costs and the benefits of each option.

- Write down the options you wish to consider. For example:
  Wait for promotion in my present job.
  Seek a more senior position in a similar department in another company.
  Transfer to another department in my present company and change my direction.

- Write the first option at the top of a sheet of paper. Divide the page down the middle and head the column on the left "Costs" and the one on the right "Benefits" (see diagram on the next page).

- Enter in the "Costs" column any disadvantages you (or others) can think of if you were to pursue that option. When you have finished listing all of the costs you can think of, read back through the list. Attempt to grade each cost on a 1 to 10 scale as an indication of how you feel about the prospect. You should rate an item 1 if you think it is a very slight disadvantage, 10 if it feels like a major disadvantage. Score the rest in between. Finally, put a circle around the two biggest disadvantages.

- Now move to the "Benefits" column under your first option and list any gains you might make from choosing that option. Grade the benefits on a 1 to 10 scale—1 if it feels only slightly advantageous, 10 if it feels to be highly advantageous to you. Score the rest in between. Finally put a circle around the two most attractive advantages from your point of view.

- Repeat this process for each option.

| Cost-Benefit Analysis (Example) | | | |
|---|---|---|---|
| **Option: Waiting for promotion** | | | |
| Costs | Rating | Benefits | Rating |
| No change of scene | 2 | I know the job and can do it well | ⑦ |
| No change of people | 5 | | |
| Lack of challenge | 8 | Little stress | 3 |
| May wait in vain | 8 | The company knows my strengths | 3 |
| Feeling helpless | ⑨ | I need to move house | ⑧ |
| Someone else might beat me to it | ⑨ | | |

- Place your cost/benefit balance sheets alongside each other.
- Examine, think about, or talk through your reactions to looking at each sheet again.
- Ask yourself, whether any option seems to give you most of what you want.
- If it does, decide whether the costs of it are acceptable to you. If so, begin to make it happen!
- If there is no option that is clearly better for you than another, then you have to either (a) postpone the decision or (b) risk choosing one option when there is no clearcut choice.
- Write down, or declare what you have decided.

Note: It can be useful to think through "What happens if I do nothing or fail to make a decision?" Sometimes the consequences of inertia are not considered!

Keep a Record

The results of your cost-benefit analysis

## Rainbow Building Progress Check

## How Do I Make Them Happen?

Using the techniques outlined, collect together all your objectives and make them as clear as possible. Look back through your "Aha!" folder.

_____

_____

_____

_____

_____

_____

_____

_____

_____

_____

_____

_____

_____

_____

# Action Planning

When you have a clearly defined objective the next step is to develop an action plan.

An action plan provides you with the answer to the question:

     What do I do to achieve my objective?

The steps in action planning are as follows:

1. Have a clearly defined objective.

   Too many action plans fail because the objective is not clear enough in the first place.

2. Start with what you are going to do now.

   The following diagram graphically portrays how action plans can fail if you try to change too much or plan too far ahead.

| | Me | You | Us | Another Group | The Organi- zation | The System | Society |
|---|---|---|---|---|---|---|---|
| Now | Firm Ground | | | | | | |
| Tomorrow | | | | | | | |
| Soon | | | | | | | |
| Sometime | | | | | | | |
| Eventually | | | | | | | |
| Never | | | | | | | |

3. Be very specific about the steps you will take to achieve your objective.

For example, not, "I'll have a chat with my boss" but, "I will try to see my boss on Thursday to discuss my current job performance and ask about ways in which I might get a promotion."

4. Arrange the action steps in a logical flow laid out so that even a computer could understand it!

5. Be aware that one action step will often require planning a prior one.

   For example, "I will telephone the boss's secretary this afternoon to arrange an appointment for Thursday morning."

6. Decide when you will review your progress and write this into your action plan.

7. Transfer your plan to a calendar to remind you of the particular dates by which the steps need to have been completed. Contracting with others is particularly useful to ensure that you are sticking to an action plan.

8. Always be prepared to change the plan as circumstances change or if some of your steps do not turn out as you have wished.

## Exercise 36: My Action Plan*

Rainbow Building Skills: Set Objectives, Make Action Plans

Take one of your objectives and develop an action plan for it.

My objective is to

_____

_____

_____

_____

_____

_____

_____

What I need to do is

_____

_____

_____

_____

_____

_____

_____


List the most useful action steps without worrying about their sequence.

_____

_____

_____

_____

_____

_____

_____


Now number them according to which comes first.

I am going to start with Step 1 on _____ (give date)

I am going to start with Step 2 on _____ (give date)

I will review my progress on _____ (give date)

I should know whether my objective
has been reached or not by _____ (give date)

Good Luck!

You can now return to your other objectives and produce action plans for them.

Your example of an action plan

## Exercise 37: A Letter to Myself*

Rainbow Building Skills: Set Objectives, Make Action Plans

Not to be opened until

_____

(a date six months ahead)

A particularly effective method of reviewing progress at this stage is to write a letter to yourself. Give the letter to someone who could be relied upon to post it to you exactly six months to the day after you have written it. By then you will, most likely, have forgotten all about it. Its appearance on your doormat can generate feelings ranging from delight to despair as you see just how much you have achieved or how far you have moved toward achieving your objectives.

- Spell out clearly what you hope to have achieved in the six months after writing the letter for each of your priority objectives.

One alternative would be to send yourself a photocopy of the summary sheet for this section.

# Rainbow Building Summary Sheet

## How Do I Make Them Happen?

| My major objectives are | To be achieved by | Action Plan? (Check if you have one) |
|---|---|---|
| | | |
| | | |
| | | |
| | | |
| | | |
| | | |
| | | |

## QUESTION 6

# What If It Doesn't Work Out?

We suggested earlier that as you worked through the first five questions there might be times when it would be appropriate to turn to Question 6. As you worked through the exercises you may have felt frustration over the constraints in your life which restrict your options or make the changes you want to bring about more difficult. Perhaps you felt disappointment over past opportunities missed. Even if you did find the exercises stimulating and constructive you will still need the lifeskills of coping when things don't work out for use in the rest of your life.

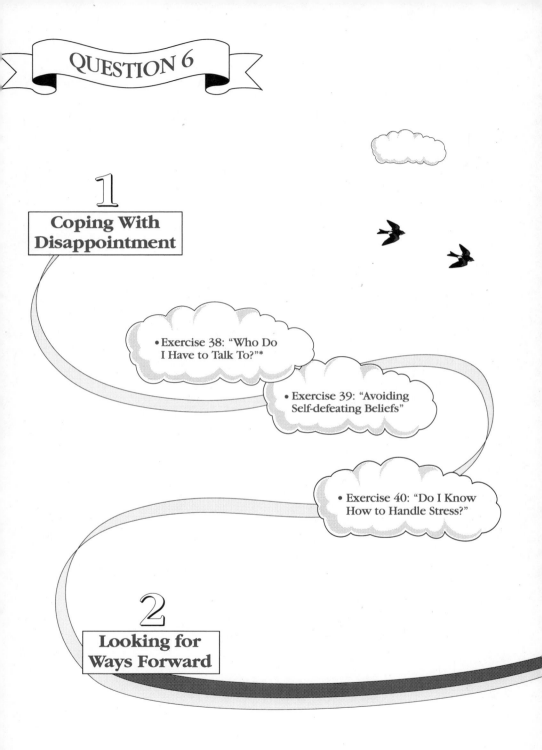

QUESTION 6

**1**

**Coping With Disappointment**

• Exercise 38: "Who Do I Have to Talk To?"*

• Exercise 39: "Avoiding Self-defeating Beliefs"

• Exercise 40: "Do I Know How to Handle Stress?"

**2**

**Looking for Ways Forward**

**\* = Essential Exercise**

# Coping With Disappointment

However clear your objectives and specific your Action Plans, however much time and energy you invest, there are always some factors outside your control that could result in your not getting what you want.

> When I finally got the means to an end, they moved the ends further apart.
>
> Sam Levinson

In addition, you do make mistakes! Your aims might not be realistic, your skills insufficiently developed, or you may even change your mind!

Taking the risk of succeeding requires that you also risk failure. The alternative would seem to be to sit tight and let life happen to you. That way you can stay out of the rainstorm, but you won't have a chance to build a rainbow.

Although you can, through successful career and life management, keep your disappointments to a minimum, you cannot expect all of your plans and projects to succeed. And when you are disappointed, you aren't in the mood to hear, "You can learn more from your mistakes than from your successes." When plans do not work out, you need to sound off about your feelings of disappointment, frustration, and anger. After dealing with your feelings, you can learn a great deal by looking back and analyzing what went wrong and by considering alternative steps you could have taken or by recognizing the skills you lacked at the time.

It is helpful to acknowledge that not all of your plans will work out and to have suitable strategies ready for coping at these times. We avoid using the word failure because too many people apply the word to themselves rather than to their plans. It can be helpful to recognize "Yes, this particular plan of mine failed," but it's extremely self-destructive to think "I am a failure because my plan didn't work out!"

When you reach a point at which you realize things are not working out, you need to consider two questions:

- How can I cope with the disappointment?
- What else can I try?

When a plan doesn't work out there are two areas a rainbow builder has to manage: emotional and rational.

The alternative strategies we suggest later are all very well if you are feeling strong and rational, but that is often the last thing you feel when you have to face a major disappointment.

The emotional reactions, for most people, will have to be dealt with first.

How do you feel when faced with great disappointment?

- Think back to a particular disappointment in your life. It may help to write down the details.
- Recall your first reactions. How did you feel? What did you feel like doing?
- To what extent were these the typical feelings you have in response to disappointments?
- Now think about what you actually do at these times. List the typical things that you do when you face disappointment.

Coping with disappointment will usually involve one or a combination of the following:

- Getting rid of bad feelings
- Having someone to talk to
- Talking constructively to yourself
- Looking after yourself under stress

Look back at your responses above. Which of these four did you use?

## Getting Rid of Bad Feelings

Crying, shouting, gardening, going for a run or a swim, and working out are all common ways in which people do this. Keeping these feelings inside you or, even worse, not admitting the disappointment to yourself will generate bad feelings, increase stress, and make the disappointment more difficult to cope with.

Now that you've thought about it a bit more, do the ways you typically cope with disappointment allow you to get rid of the bad feelings? Which of these suggestions might you try another time? Can you think of others that might particularly suit you?

## Having Someone to Talk To

A problem for many of us is that we often expect most of our support and emotional sustenance from one or two people. We sometimes act as if it is wholly reasonable to expect to get all of our needs satisfied by a single person—usually a spouse, a member of one's immediate family, or one or two close friends. The following exercise will help you to identify just who is in your support network while making the point that support is a many faceted thing. You do have a choice to extend it, plug gaps, and make changes.

### Exercise 38: Who Do I Have to Talk To?*

Rainbow Building Skill: Look After Yourself

Write in the names of people you know who provide you with these different kinds of support in your job and away from your job.

| My Support Network | | |
|---|---|---|
| Types of Support | At My Job | Away From My Job |
| Someone I can always rely on | | |
| Someone I just enjoy talking to | | |
| Someone with whom I can discuss the exercises in this book | | |
| Someone who makes me feel competent and valued | | |
| Someone who gives me constructive feedback | | |
| Someone who is always a valuable source of information | | |
| Someone who will challenge me to take a good look at myself | | |

| My Support Network (continued) | | |
|---|---|---|
| Types of Support | At My Job | Away From My Job |
| Someone I can depend upon in a crisis | | |
| Someone I can feel close to—a friend or intimate | | |
| Someone I can share bad news with | | |
| Someone I can share good news and good feelings with | | |
| Someone who introduces me to new ideas, new interests, new people | | |

Does anything surprise me when I look at the extent of my support network?

Are there any gaps?

Do I rely on only one or two people for my support? Does this matter? What are the consequences of this for me and for them?

Do I wish to change my support network in any way?

Your answers to the last question should be kept with your previous work on Section 4: "What Changes Do I Want?" in your "Aha!" folder.

It is sometimes difficult to feel that you can ask for support. However, most people are happy to offer it. It helps, too, if you make a practice of seeking support periodically rather than bottling things up. Then you will not find it so difficult to approach people when you do have to cope with major disappointments. For most people, offering support is a two-way process: They willingly give support and hope to receive it when they need it.

Some people feel it's important to keep their problems to themselves and manage on their own so as not to bother other people. But, since most people like to be asked for help when it's really needed, such an attitude could be seen as either misplaced pride or as a signal that the person feels worthless or doesn't deserve help.

If you find it difficult to identify people to whom you could turn, go back to the "Personal Contact Network" you created in Exercise 31 and find those people not in your immediate circle of friends who could offer appropriate support if asked.

**Keep a Record**

- Your support network
- Observations and Action Plans

It's always possible that because of the nature of the problem, or because you are away from home or have moved, that you may not be able to think of anyone who could help. In this case, check the Social Services listings in your telephone book for referrals in your area.

## Talking Constructively to Yourself

This skill is crucial when things do not turn out well for you. The way you think is likely to have a highly significant influence on the way you feel and what you do. The way you perceive a given situation, what you "tell yourself" as you think about it, will have a decisive effect on what feelings you experience and your consequent actions.

Typically when an unfortunate event or experience occurs, you feel bad and assume that your feelings are created by that event.

What actually happens, however, is that something comes between the event and the feelings that will determine just what kind of feelings you experience. We call that "something" self-talk. This determines how you experience any event, which in turn will determine what you feel and ultimately how you act.

The real sequence, therefore, is as follows:

For example: This was one person's reaction to failing a driving test.

Event:          This person's objective was to pass his driving test, but
                he failed.

Self-talk:      I'm pathetic. Anyone can pass a driving test. I'm a fail-
                ure. I'm not going to risk looking stupid again.

Feelings:       He felt ashamed, frustrated, pathetic.

This is how it can affect, in turn, the fourth factor in our equation:

Actions:        Since he did not want to experience those feelings
                again, he was determined not to put himself at risk.
                He was not going to try again.

All of this stems from assuming that your feelings are caused directly
by the event, whereas they are determined almost totally by how you
talk to yourself and interpret the event.

Before the feelings stage the person above could substitute the
following self-talk:

"I am disappointed. It would have been good to have passed, especially because I practiced so hard. However, things don't always turn
out as we wish. I have failed but that doesn't make me a failure. I have
to see how I can learn from my mistakes so that next time I won't
repeat them."

Think of what you did when facing a disappointment. Did you use
negative self-talk then? If so, what might you have said that would be
more positive? It is important, therefore, in terms of looking after
yourself to realize that

- What you *think* will decide what you feel and do.
- If you can control what you think, you can manage your feelings
  and your behavior more effectively.
- If you do this, you can take greater charge of yourself and the
  situations you meet.

Realizing this is the first step to learning the kind of self-talk that will
promote looking after yourself and will reduce the likelihood or your
being a "victim" of bad feelings or of situations that you cannot control.

## Exercise 39: Avoiding Self-defeating Beliefs

Rainbow Building Skill: Communicate

Contrary to what you might believe, other people or things do not make you unhappy. You make yourself unhappy by what you tell yourself. Train yourself to avoid negative or destructive self-talk and particularly to avoid thoughts that are based on self-defeating beliefs. These beliefs set up unrealistic expectations of yourself, of other people, or of the world and invite disappointment.

These beliefs lead to most of the feelings of worry, anger, fear, jealousy, depression, and guilt that people experience. If you believe them you will think in terms of "Things should be..." or, "People ought to be..." and you will get angry or disappointed a great deal of the time when events or people do not live up to your expectations. If you can begin to accept that there are no "shoulds" and "oughts" and begin to think in terms of "It would be preferable if..." or, "I may need to work to bring that about," then you will be more likely to act to make things more like you want them to be.

The following is a list of some beliefs that are likely to produce problems. As you read the list, circle the number of any to which you always or sometimes subscribe.

1. I must be loved or liked by everyone; people should love me.
2. I must be perfect in all I do.
3. All the people with whom I work or live must be perfect.
4. I can have little control over what happens to me.
5. It is easier to avoid facing difficulties than to deal with them.
6. Disagreement and conflict are to be avoided at all costs.
7. People, including me, do not change.
8. Some people are always good; others are always bad.
9. The world should be perfect and it is terrible and unbearable that it is not.
10. People are fragile and need to be protected from "the truth."
11. Other people make me happy; I cannot be happy without them.
12. Crises are destructive and no good can come from them.
13. Somewhere there is the perfect job, the perfect solution, the perfect partner, etc., and all I need to do is search for them.
14. I should not have problems; if I do it indicates I am incompetent.
15. There is only one way of seeing any situation.

- Remember the last time you felt bad about something—angry, jealous, or resentful. What were you telling yourself? Were any of these fifteen beliefs the basis for your self-talk?
- Now, you are going to challenge the destructive self-talk that caused you those difficulties. Fill in the table for the event you have just thought about. Write down your self-destructive talk in your own words. Your self-talk may well include condemnation of yourself and be full of what people should or ought to do.

| *My Self-defeating Belief* |
| --- |
| The event: |
| What I felt: |
| What I was telling myself: |
| What it made me do: |
| What my self-defeating belief was: |

- Now challenge that self-talk and reinterpret it by exchanging the shoulds and oughts for preferences. Talk to yourself about what you can learn from the experience. Tell yourself that you can behave differently next time.

- Fill in the table below with alternative constructive self-talk and the consequences that could have resulted.

| Constructive self-talk |
| --- |
| Feelings would be |
| Actions could be |

If you can

1. Avoid self-defeating thinking when difficulties arise; and
2. Develop ways of thinking (using self-talk) based on a more rational approach in times of difficulty;

you will be more likely to manage yourself and the situation more effectively when things do not turn out as you wish.

There may be times when self-defeating talk becomes almost obsessional: you can't get such thoughts out of your mind. Here you have to try something that might sound silly but works—tell yourself firmly to "stop" whenever you catch yourself doing it. Don't make it worse by thinking "You are stupid to feel like that." That's just more self-defeating talk. Just "stop" and then move on to positive self-talk. Have some positive thoughts or pictures ready to put into your head automatically. You can work steadily toward giving up all your self-defeating beliefs.

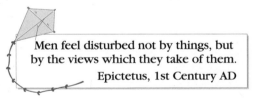

Men feel disturbed not by things, but by the views which they take of them.
Epictetus, 1st Century AD

When you are under stress you may find that your favorite negative self-talk—usually the one that allows you to say something rotten to yourself about yourself—creeps back into your mind. This could be a sign to you that you need to pay more attention to your stress levels and to looking after yourself.

## *Looking After Yourself Under Stress*

Research has consistently shown that the fitter you are, the more energy you have to cope with the problems that arise and disappointments that are inevitable in everyday life. Keeping fit will help to prevent undue stress when things do not go well for you. Also when you do experience the ill effects of stress, physical exercise can help you to feel better.

The other side to looking after yourself physically is to learn to relax when all around you is movement, turmoil, frustration, and disappointment. There are many ways of relaxing and perhaps it appears strange to read of this as a skill.

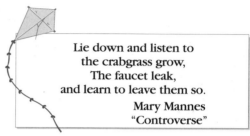

Lie down and listen to
the crabgrass grow,
The faucet leak,
and learn to leave them so.
Mary Mannes
"Controverse"

It is important for everyone to discover the techniques that work for them. Some people are totally incapable of relaxing. Below are some techniques for relaxation.

Techniques that work directly on our bodies

- Meditation
- Progressive relaxation
- Deep breathing
- Yoga
- Massage

Techniques that work indirectly through a psychological process

- Listening to music
- Reading a book, watching TV
- Having a drink
- Going to a peaceful place
- Being with people you can be yourself with

Stimulation as a way of relaxation

Sometimes when you are tired you don't feel like doing anything. Hard work can make you tired so that you physically need a rest. However, when high stress makes you feel tired, switching to a stimulating activity can make you feel better and full of energy again. It helps to think about what is behind your tiredness. You could try the following:

- A brisk walk
- A quick shower rather than a relaxing soak in the bath
- Dancing to a favorite song
- Phoning a friend
- Making a spontaneous decision to go out somewhere (meal, film, bowling, bingo, roller skating). Try something different!

Which of the options in this list have you tried? Do they work for you? Which others might you try?

Your list of self-defeating beliefs and what you can do to counter them

## Exercise 40: Do I Know How to Handle Stress?

Rainbow Building Skill: Look After Yourself

When your plans (even the subconscious ones) do not work out, you can easily feel under a considerable amount of stress as a result. Below are listed a variety of questions about "looking after yourself" in stressful situations.

Check the statements to which you can answer "Yes."

( ) Do I get regular exercise, or follow a personal fitness program?
( ) Do I eat regularly and have a balanced diet?
( ) Do I keep to a regular schedule?
( ) Do I know how to say "No" to things I don't want, and conversely, do I know how to ask for what I do want?
( ) Do I give myself a break, or some kind of a "treat" when under stress?

( ) Do I have people to whom I can turn for help?
( ) Do I actually turn to them?
( ) Do I know how to relax?
( ) Do I talk constructively to myself?

If you scored 7–8 you should cope with disappointment well.

If you scored 4–6 you can cope with some disappointment but would benefit by developing your "looking after yourself" skills.

If you scored 0–3 you are likely to be incapacitated by disappointment unless you make definite plans to acquire better "looking after yourself" skills.

Look in the Resources section for materials that are broadly concerned with "looking after yourself." Most of these should be available in your local library. In addition to books, you could enroll in such classes as yoga, meditation, relaxation, massage, assertiveness, fitness, and time management. Your local library, newspaper, and community colleges are good places to find out what is going on in your area.

## Looking for Ways Forward

When you have coped effectively with your feelings of disappointment, you are free to use your skills of rational thinking to help work out what to do next.

If things do not work out as you wish

1. Reappraise your action plan.
2. If that does not work, reappraise your original objectives.
3. Ask why it didn't work. What was due to your influence? What was due to external influences?
4. Ask yourself what you can learn from the experience.
5. Always have a backup plan (Plan B). Develop it alongside Plan A and try to identify check points during Plan A at which you can review progress and if necessary cut your losses and switch to Plan B. Your original plan should be flexible enough for you to

be able to revise and improve it as you go along and to enable you to switch to Plan B if you need to.

By all means put everything you've got in to achieving Plan A, but don't let the chance to reach your goal fall through because you haven't taken the time to consider other ways of reaching it.

6. Take a lateral step. Consider a different goal if your first choice proves unobtainable.

Whenever you are in a situation that you wish to change there are always four basic strategies for managing that situation. They are illustrated in the figure below.

**2. Leave**

**1. Change the Situation**  **3. Change Yourself**

**4. Creatively Live With It**

### Strategy 1: Change the Situation

The first strategy is often that of trying to change the situation to make it more like you want it to be. However, having tried to make changes to no avail, you are left with the other three options.

### Strategy 2: Leave

You exit from the situation, job, relationship, or problem.

### Strategy 3: Change Yourself

Perhaps if you changed your ambitions, attitude, behavior, lifestyle, or whatever, your situation would improve.

### Strategy 4: Creatively Live With It

This means much more than simply, "Putting up with it." It requires a conscious strategy so that you can minimize the undesirable aspects of the situation and maximize the desirable ones. Examples might include investing more energy in activities outside of your job (if dissatisfied at work), isolating yourself in a project in such a way that it reduces your contact with troublesome elements, or spending more time doing the things you enjoy and cutting down on the others.

Below is an example worked out by someone who was extremely dissatisfied with her job.

### Change the Situation

Options

- Suggest a new project
- Negotiate for a redefinition of my job
- Suggest that meetings be more structured
- Ask for salary increase
- Arrange to work more with people I like

### Leave

Options

- Get new job
- Get leave of absence
- Get industrial sabbatical
- Take early retirement
- Get transfer to another site

### Change Yourself

Options

- Lower my expectations
- Get retrained
- Undertake inservice training

### Creatively Live With It

Options

- Focus more on other areas of my life
- Go part-time
- Take a second job
- Take an adult education course

Things won't always work out, you will make mistakes, others will block your goals. The challenge for you is how well you react to that.

# Rainbow Building Summary Sheet

## What If It Doesn't Work Out?

1. List the techniques you use to deal with disappointment.
   Add new ones you are going to try.

Physical:

_____

_____

_____

Psychological:

_____

_____

_____

List the key people in your support network:

_____

_____

_____

2. Which "looking after yourself" skills do you need to improve or acquire?

   a. _____

   b. _____

   c. _____

What are the next steps you have to take in order to do this?

   a. _____

   b. _____

   c. _____

3. List your most common self-defeating beliefs.

    a. _____

    b. _____

    c. _____

Translate each of them into more positive self-talk.

    a. _____

    b. _____

    c. _____

# At the End of
# Your Rainbow

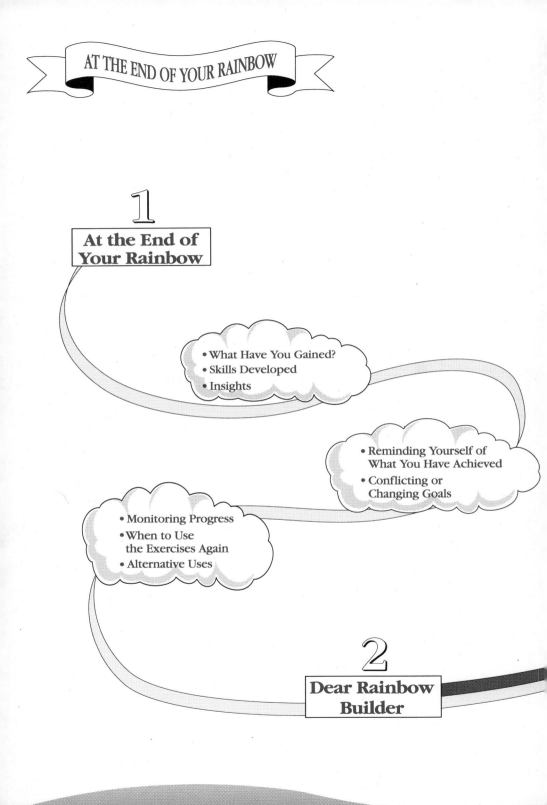

**1**

At the End of
Your Rainbow

- What Have You Gained?
- Skills Developed
- Insights

- Reminding Yourself of
  What You Have Achieved
- Conflicting or
  Changing Goals

- Monitoring Progress
- When to Use
  the Exercises Again
- Alternative Uses

**2**

Dear Rainbow
Builder

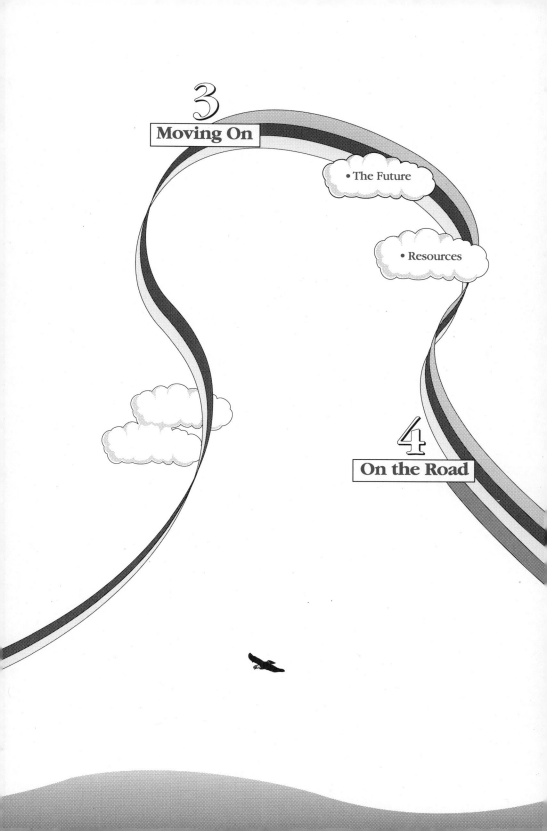

3
Moving On

• The Future

• Resources

4
On the Road

# At the End of Your Rainbow

We have reached the end of our rainbow building program. How useful has it been for you? This book offers you the chance to find out about yourself. It can tell you how to do it but only you can do the hard work involved. Return to the contract you made with us on page 29. How well have you stuck to the contract?

In part 4 of the contract you were asked to identify ways you have sabotaged yourself in the past. Did you catch yourself doing it this time? Are you now more aware of the ways in which you do it? For example did you:

- Skim through the book meaning to come back and actually do the exercises—but didn't?
- Only start reading when you were too tired?
- Never allocate sufficient time to do enough work on it?
- Defeat yourself by negative self-talk and turn every exercise into an opportunity to put yourself down?
- Use any of the devices above to avoid acknowledging that it can be quite scary to explore yourself in this way?

We are not in a position to challenge you on this: but we are asking you to challenge yourself.

## What Have You Gained?

You can review what you have achieved by looking through the notes you have made and at the progress checks and summary sheets.

Sum up what has proved most important for you in each of these three areas:

1. Information (facts) I've learned:

_____

_____

_____

_____

_____

_____

_____

_____

## 2. Skills I've developed:

_____

_____

_____

_____

_____

_____

## 3. Insights I've gained (Look through you "Aha" folder):

_____

_____

_____

_____

_____

_____

_____

## Skills Developed

At the start of this book we said a rainbow builder needs to develop seven types of skills. The whole range has been covered but "Know Yourself" has been the main focus of the exercise. As a rainbow builder you need to have a thorough understanding of your raw materials.

The following table sums up which skills the various exercises have been helping you to build. Which of the exercises have proved most useful to you? Put a check in the skills columns opposite the exercises to indicate in which way you found each exercise to be helpful.

| Exercise | Know Yourself | Research Skills | Learn from Experience | Communicate | Make Decisions | Make Action Plans | Set Objectives | Look After Yourself |
|---|---|---|---|---|---|---|---|---|
| 1. Drawing My Lifeline | | | | | | | | |
| 2. How Do I Spend My Time | | | | | | | | |
| 3-9. Values Clarification Exercises | | | | | | | | |
| 10. Finding My Transferable Skills | | | | | | | | |
| 11. What Are My Interests? | | | | | | | | |
| 12. Choosing Where to Live | | | | | | | | |
| 13. The Ages of Me | | | | | | | | |
| 14. What Life Stages Am I at Now? | | | | | | | | |

| Exercise | Know Yourself | Research Skills | Learn from Experience | Communicate | Make Decisions | Make Action Plans | Set Objectives | Look After Yourself |
|---|---|---|---|---|---|---|---|---|
| 15-17. Career Pattern Exercises | | | | | | | | |
| 18. How Do Others See You? | | | | | | | | |
| 19. Analyzing My Time | | | | | | | | |
| 20. Analyzing My Satisfaction | | | | | | | | |
| 21. My Career and Life Mind Map | | | | | | | | |
| 22. My Fantasy Job (Career, Life, or Day) | | | | | | | | |
| 23. Complaints into Objectives | | | | | | | | |
| 24. This Is Your Life . . . Continued | | | | | | | | |
| 25. Let Me Introduce Myself | | | | | | | | |
| 26. My Future Life Roles | | | | | | | | |
| 27. My Obituary | | | | | | | | |
| 28. What I Earn, Spend, and Need | | | | | | | | |

| Exercise | Know Yourself | Research Skills | Learn from Experience | Communicate | Make Decisions | Make Action Plans | Set Objectives | Look After Yourself |
|---|---|---|---|---|---|---|---|---|
| 29. My Monkey Trap | | | | | | | | |
| 30. Buy Me Today | | | | | | | | |
| 31. Who Do I Know? | | | | | | | | |
| 32. More of/ Less of Matrix | | | | | | | | |
| 33. 12 Steps Toward Clear Objectives | | | | | | | | |
| 34. Force-Field Analysis | | | | | | | | |
| 35. Cost-Benefit Analysis | | | | | | | | |
| 36. My Action Plan | | | | | | | | |
| 37. A Letter to Myself | | | | | | | | |
| 38. Who Do I Have to Talk To? | | | | | | | | |
| 39. Avoiding Self-defeating Beliefs | | | | | | | | |
| 40. Do I Know How to Look After Myself Under Stress? | | | | | | | | |

Now consider the following:

- Are there some exercises you left out that you would like to go back to?
- Do you wish to repeat some of the exercises?
- Which of the seven skills do you want to build up?

## Insights

In the future these may be your most vivid memories of working through this book. Insights are usually gained when we are thinking most deeply about ourselves—it's almost as if we have dredged them up. However it sometimes seems as if we find them too painful—or challenging, and they sink down again out of sight. We forget the insights we have gained.

You can help prevent this from happening and gain most from them by taking each of the key insights you have just listed (page 212) and writing some action notes for them. Will you now be on the alert for certain situations to which you will try to react differently? Do you want to change yourself in any way? Or perhaps acknowledge and accept the person you now see yourself to be?

## Reminding Yourself of What You Have Achieved

Working through this book should have proved challenging and stimulating. It may at times have been hard work or painful. It's quite an achievement to have examined your life in this way. You should feel proud of yourself. Praise yourself—it's better than praise from others! You might like to write yourself a postcard noting exactly what you are proud of having done. You could pin it up picture side out where you can see it regularly. It will remind you of what's on the other side.

## Conflicting or Changing Goals?

The Rainbow Building Summary Sheet you completed at the end of Question 5 may well have identified for you that some of your goals conflict. Or you may realize that pursuing some of your goals would conflict with the goals of those you live or work with. This will probably mean that you need to reconsider the priority you give to the various values you have already looked at. You may also need to move on to consider what your values are for personal relationships and for involvement and responsibilities within the community and society.

You've probably already found that at different times in your life you have chosen or been forced to give priority to different goals. It may well be the same in the future. Your action plans will need to take this into account. Try making short-term and medium-term action plans:

1. Short-term—What will you achieve during the next six months?
2. Medium-term—What, at this moment, do you hope to achieve during the next five years? If you review this plan every year you will have a rolling five year plan that can be more responsive to the changing priorities you may need to give to your goals.

An additional strategy is to keep an updated list of what you hope to achieve before the end of your life. The list will certainly change as the balance of your values shift at successive life stages: Doing this can spur you on to make life happen, rather than to let life happen to you. However, there is a danger that you will suddenly go from thinking, "There's plenty of time to fit everything in," to "Good heavens time is running out." If this happens you'll probably then recognize that it counts as a "midlife turning point" and that you should go through this Life Management Review again.

## Monitoring Progress

You may decide to repeat some of these exercises either regularly or at certain times, especially if major changes are coming up. They can be used as a way of quality control monitoring for your life. You could make a note in your planning calendar to check through this list during the last days of December when you are getting yourself together to face a new year. On the next page are some suggestions as to how you might use them.

# When to Use the Exercises Again

| Exercise | When to Use |
|---|---|
| Exercise 2: How Do I Spend My Time? plus Exercises 19 and 20 | Regular review: demands and needs will vary<br><br>When you are under pressure.<br><br>When you feel increasingly tired.<br><br>When you are having trouble meeting new committments. |
| Exercises 7, 8, and 9, values and needs | At different life stages (see Exercise 14) when priorities are likely to change (about every five years).<br><br>When certain life events challenge your values. |
| Exercise 10: Finding My Transferable Skills | Keep this updated (particularly if you want to keep an up-to-date résumé, but also as a morale-booster). |
| Exercise 11: What are My Interests? | Check occasionally—your energies and enthusiasms may vary.<br><br>Do it to challenge yourself to try new things and to check if those you are saving up for later in life ever get done. |
| Exercise 14: Life Stages | Check every five years. |
| Exercise 17: A Dual Career Family | Do this when relevant. |
| Exercise 18: How Do Others See Me? | Occasionally—if you begin to suspect that your image of yourself needs adjustment in the light of feedback from other people. |
| Exercise 21: My Life and Career Mind Map | Use to monitor changes in your "satisfiers" and "dissatisfiers." |
| Exercise 26: My Future Life Roles | Check in ten years to see if you were right! |

| Exercise | When to Use |
|---|---|
| Exercise 31: Who Do I Know? | Review and revise—this will alert you to where you are losing contact with parts of your network. Do you want to lose contact?<br><br>Are you adding new people? |
| Exercise 32: More of/Less of Matrix | Monitor progress and make new action plans periodically. |
| Exercise 37: A Letter to Myself | Remember to open it! |
| Exercise 38: Who Do I Have to Talk To? | Monitor regularly to see that you do.<br><br>Check when under stress since these are the people who can best support you. |
| Exercise 40: Do I Know How to Look After Myself Under Stress? | This needs to be kept up all your life. Six-month reviews will help. |

## Alternative Uses

The exercises have been developed to help you look at life and career management, but you can adapt them to other issues that you want to examine or projects that you want to plan.

Many of them can be used at transition times when you are facing major changes in your life. You may have chosen to make the change and enjoy doing it but the ripple effect of the change on the whole of your life and the people in it make it a stressful time.

Here are some other ideas for two other areas of life:

### *Marriage*

- Exercises 1 and 24 can be adapted to explore the history and possible future of your marriage. Both partners should draw their own future life lines and discuss them with one another.
- Exercise 6: What I Want From Play/Leisure and Exercises 2, 19 and 20 may help both partners negotiate new understandings between them. So will Exercise 32: More of/Less of Matrix.

- Exercise 17 "A Dual Career" could be done before marriage as well as at various stages during the marriage.
- Exercise 22—Think about your fantasy partner and fantasy marriage. What does this tell you about yourself? What would be appropriate for you to share with your partner?

## *Consumer and Political Action*

- Exercise 23: Complaints Into Objectives is probably the starting point.
- Exercise 31: Who Do I Know? When members of a group pool the relevant parts of their networks supportive and influential people can usually be found.
- Exercise 33: 12 Steps Toward Clear Objectives, Exercise 34: Force-Field Analysis, and Exercise 36: My Action Plan will help you develop a campaign.
- Exercise 35: Cost-Benefit Analysis can help you see pros and cons of a proposed action or choose between options.

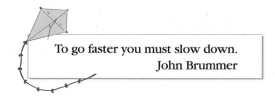

To go faster you must slow down.
John Brummer

# Dear Rainbow Builder

The skills you have learned are transferable. You can go on building rainbows.

Before you move on, please accept this award with our congratulations for completing this program!

With these skills you will go far!

# Moving On

## The Future

This program can be hard work. We would suggest that before you move on you relax, take a break, and go and have some fun. Then come back and think about your plans for the future. Here are some suggestions you might try.

Your plans might include the following:

- Seeking out more information
- Building up your life skills
- Gaining more insights into yourself

Which areas?

Here are a few you might choose from:

- Further work/career management
- Personal relationships
- Looking after yourself
- Leisure interests
- Management skills
- Unpaid work options
- Planning for early retirement

## Resources

Your choice may depend on whether you want to concentrate on information, skills, or insights. Consider which of these you might want to use:

### Books

In general they are good for information. "How-to-do-it" books for skills. "How-to-do-it" human psychology books for insights as well as skills. Ask your library for help in getting relevant book lists.

## Counseling/Advice

Ask at library or refer to the Community Services listings in your local yellow pages directory for what's available in your area.

Consider using career counselors, marriage counselors—who accept any life-review concern as a suitable reason for seeking help, or psychotherapy (ask your physician for his or her recommendation of what you may need and who you could see).

## Local Classes

You may need direct personal tutoring for learning certain skills. Being able to share your experiences with others is an additional benefit. Check local newspapers, libraries, and Commuinity Colleges for further information.

> People travel to wonder at the height of mountains, at the huge waves of the sea, at the long courses of rivers, at the vast compass of the ocean, at the circular motion of the stars; and they pass by themselves without wondering.
>
> St. Augustine

# On the Road

Now that you have completed the exercises contained in this book, you have a good idea of the direction you want your career to go. The options available to improve your current situation should be more apparant, and the path you need to take to achieve this improvement is more clear. Some of you, however, may have found that a complete change of situation is what you really want. You know where you want to go, and have the skills it takes to get there. These are the crucial steps you have taken on the road to successfully building your rainbow.

Lets review for a moment the lifeskills you have uncovered.

1. Know Yourself—your values, interests, transferrable skills, your life stage, and your current life situation
2. Research Skills—obtaining knowledge about yourself by looking inward, and the ability to access external information from a variety of sources
3. Learn From Your Experience—the ability to analyze a past experience and identify what was learned from it in order to be better prepared to face a similar situation in the future
4. Communicate—expressing yourself clearly, listening carefully, and interacting effectively with other people
5. Make Decisions—using strategies you have developed to generate alternative choices from information presented to you, and selecting the most appropriate choice for your goals
6. Set Objectives, Make Action Plans—making concrete, achievable objectives from your general life aims and setting up a plan of action to achieve each specific objective
7. Look After Yourself—using stress management, stress prevention, and active relaxation techniques to add quality to your life

These skills will help you build your rainbow. So pull out your action plan and get to work on accomplishing the tasks you have set out for yourself!

# Appendix 1: Occupations Index

## ADMINISTRATIVE OCCUPATIONS

Occupations whose principal activities include making decisions, coordinating activities, supervising workers, and providing administrative staff services. Occupations are included here if their principle activity is managment rather than production.

## General Administrative

### *Restaurant Managers*

Food Service Managers
Fast-Food Service Managers
Cafeteria Managers
Food Services Directors

### *Hotel and Motel Managers*

Lodging Facilities Managers
Convention Managers
Hotel Recreation Facilities Managers
Front Office Managers

### *Health Service Administrators*

Hospital Administrators
Institution Directors
Nursing Service Directors

Emergency Medical Services Coordinators
Medical Records Administrators

### *Education Administrators*

Principals
School Superintendents
Education Institution Presidents
Academic Deans
Deans of Students
Registrars
Directors of Admissions
Financial Aid Officers
Educational Program Directors
Institutitional Research Directors
Student Affairs Directors

### *Public Administrators*

Legislators
Human Resources Program Administrators
Rural, Urban, and Community Development Program Administrators
Judicial, Public Safety, and Corrections Administrators
Natural Resources Program Administrators
Public Finance, Taxation, and Other Monetary Program Administrators
City Managers
Postmasters
Housing Management Officers

## Small Business Operators

### Business Executives

Corporate Presidents
Corporate Vice-Presidents
Financial Institution Presidents

### Financial Managers

College or University Business
  Managers
Controllers
Treasurers
Bank Officers and Managers
Budget Officers
Credit Union Managers

### Construction Superintendents

General Building Contractors
General Engineering Contractors
Bridges and Buildings
  Superintendents
Construction Inspectors
Construction Supervisors

### Production Superintendents

General Supervisors
Plant Managers
Labor Utilization Superintendents
Maintenance Superintendents
Electric Power Superintendents

### Corporate Managers

Program Managers
Operations Managers
Department Managers
Project Directors
Research and Development Directors

Property Managers
Communications Operations
  Managers
Transportation Facilities and Opera-
  tions Managers
Electricity, Gas, Water Supply, and
  Sanitary Services Managers
Electronics Data Processing Directors

### Sales and Service Managers

Retail Store Managers
Automobile Service Department
  Managers
Parts Managers
Merchandise Managers
Department Managers

### Military Officers

Logistics Officers
Planning Officers
Intelligence Officers

## Administrative Staff

### Buyers and Purchasing Agents

Retail and Wholesale Buyers
Purchasing Agents
Farm Products Purchasing Agents
  and Buyers
Purchase Price Analysts
Contracts Managers

### Personnel Officers

Personnel Managers
Labor Relations Managers
Employment Managers
Job Analysts
Employment Interviewers

Compensation Managers
Benefits Managers
Education and Training Managers
Recruiters
Placement Directors

## Public Relations Workers

Public Relations Representatives
Sales and Service Promoters
Fundraising Directors
Lobbyists
Promotion Managers
Advertising Managers

# AGRICULTURE, FORESTRY, AND FISHERY OCCUPATIONS

Occupations in which workers plan and work to get increased production from farms, gardens, forests, streams, and oceans.

## Forestry

### Park Rangers

Snow Rangers
Park Superintendents

### Foresters

Forestry and Conservation Scientists
Forest Ecologists
Silviculturists
Wood Technologists

### Fish and Wildlife Technicians

Aquatic Technicians

Fish Hatchery Workers
Gamekeepers
Fish Farmers
Gamefarm Helpers

### Forestry Technicians

Forest Conservation Workers
Tree Planters
Seedling Pullers
Seedling Sorters
Forest Products Gatherers
Forestry Aides

## Horticulture

### Groundskeepers and Gardeners

Industrial and Commercial
    Groundskeepers
Parks and Grounds Groundskeepers
Landscape Gardeners
Landscape Laborers
Lawn Service Workers
Yard Workers

### Floral Designers

Floral Arrangers

## Commercial Agriculture

### Farmers and Ranchers

Farm Managers
Poultry and Egg Farmers
Livestock Ranchers
Cash Grain Farmers
Tree-Fruit and Nut Crop Farmers
Field Crop Farmers

Vegetable Farmers
Plant Propagators

### Farm and Ranch Hands

Grain Farmworkers
Vegetable Farmworkers
Fruit Farmworkers
Field Crop Farmworkers
Livestock Farmworkers
Farm-Machine Operators
Irrigation Workers
Poultry Workers
Dairy Workers
Nursery Workers
Horticultural Workers

### Seasonal Farm Laborers

Vegetable Harvest Workers
Fruit Harvest Workers
Field Crop Harvest Workers

### Animal Caretakers

Aquarists
Stable Attendants
Horseshoers
Dog Groomers
Animal Keepers
Veterinary Assistants
Horse Trainers

## Fishery

### Commercial Fishers

Net Fishers
Line Fishers
Fishing Vessel Deckhands

Fishing Vessel Captains
Fishing Vessel Mates

# ARTS AND ENTERTAINMENT OCCUPATIONS

Occupations in which workers inform or entertain people.

### Film Production Occupations

Producers
Television and Movie Directors
Film Editors
Light Technicians
Motion Picture Photographers
Grips
Rerecording Mixers
Cinematographers
Stage Hands

### Radio and Television Broadcasters

Disk Jockeys
Newscasters
Announcers
Commentators

### Fine Artists

Sculptors
Painters
Printmakers

### Models

Photographers' Models
Artists' Models

## Performing Artists

Dancers and Choreographers
Singers
Music Conductors and Directors
Composers
Instrumental Musicians
Actors and Actresses

## Professional Athletes

Basketball Players
Tennis Players
Football Players
Soccer Players
Golfers
Bowlers
Baseball Players
Automobile Racers
Motorcycle Racers
Jockeys
Umpires

# BOOKKEEPING AND ACCOUNTING OCCUPATIONS

Occupations principally involved in maintaining and processing the office records required for effective management.

## General Accounting

### Accountants and Auditors

Tax Accountants
Cost Accountants
Budget Accountants
Systems Accountants
Property Accountants
Internal Auditors
Tax Auditors
Budget Analysts
Cost Estimators

### Bookkeepers

General Ledger Bookkeepers
Account Information Clerks

### Accounting and Statistical Clerks

Payroll Clerks
Billing Clerks
Audit Clerks
Credit Card Clerks
Reconcilement Clerks
Collection Clerks
Check Processing Clerks
Balance Clerks
Interest Clerks
Posting Clerks
Voucher Clerks
Timekeepers
Cost and Rate Clerks
Budget Clerks

## Credit and Collection

### Claims Adjusters and Examiners

Insurance Adjusters
Claims Clerks
Automobile Damage Appraisers

## Appraisers

Real Estate Appraisers
Art Appraisers
Buildings Appraisers
Personal Property Appraisers
Land Appraisers
Pawnbrokers

## Underwriters

Accident and Sickness Underwriters
Automobile Underwriters
Bond Underwriters
Casualty Underwriters
Compensation Underwriters
Credit Life Underwriters
Fire Underwriters
Group Underwriters
Liability Underwriters
Life Underwriters
Marine Underwriters
Pension and Advanced Underwriting Specialists
Special Risks Underwriters
Medical Statement Approvers

## Loan Officers

Credit Analysts
Loan Counselors
Loan Interviewers
Loan Closers

## Collectors

Repossessors
Skip Tracers
Collection Clerks

## Cashiers and Grocery Checkers

Cashier Checkers
Ticket Sellers
Front Office Cashiers
Food and Beverage Order Clerks
Cashier Wrappers
Check Cashiers
Food Sales Clerks

## Bank Tellers

Collection and Exchange Tellers
Note Tellers
Head Tellers
Exchange Clerks
Drive-In Tellers
Securities Tellers

# BUILDING MAINTENANCE OCCUPATIONS

Occupations in which workers clean, repair, and maintain buildings such as schools, offices, and apartments.

## Commercial Buildings

### Building Maintenance Workers

General Utility Maintenance Repairers
Building Maintenance Repairers
Factory or Mill Maintenance Repairers

## Cleaning

### *Room Cleaners*

Housekeepers
House Cleaners
Hospital Cleaners
Light Cleaners

### *Janitors*

Industrial Cleaners
Commercial or Institutional Cleaners
Window Cleaners
Floor Waxers
Wall Cleaners
Industrial Sweepers-Cleaners
Chimney Sweeps

### *Domestic Service Workers*

General House Workers
Day Workers
Home Attendants
Caretakers
Private Household Cooks
Launderers and Ironers

# CLERICAL OCCUPATIONS

Occupations that exist principally to aid communication and the flow of business within and between organizations by typing letters, keeping files, greeting visitors, answering telephones, and helping managers.

## General Clerical

### *Office Managers*

Administrative Assistants
General Office Supervisors
Computer and Equipment Operator Supervisors
Clerical Supervisors
Financial Record Processing Supervisors
Office Machine Operator Supervisors
Communications Supervisors
Mail and Distribution Supervisors
Scheduling and Distribution Supervisors
Operations Officers

### *Stenographers*

Stenotype Operators
Technical Stenographers
Print Shop Stenographers

### *Shorthand Reporters*

Court Reporters
Hearings Reporters

### *Clerk Typists*

Typists

### *General Office Clerks*

File Clerks
Administrative Clerks
Personnel Clerks
Interviewing Clerks
Desk Clerks
Customer Services Representatives

Order Clerks
Correspondence Clerks

### Word Processing Machine Operators

Magnetic-Tape-Typewriter Operators
Photocomposition Keyboard
   Operators
Terminal System Operators

### Teacher Aides

Grading Clerks
Examination Proctors
Resource Center Aides

### Travel Agents

Travel Clerks

### Ticket Agents

Ticketing Clerks
Reservation Agents
Transportation Agents
Station Agents

### Library Assistants

Library Technical Assistants
Library Clerks
Shelving Supervisors
Pages
Registration Clerks

### Medical Records Technicians

Medical Records Clerks
Medical Transcriptionists

### Data Entry Operators

Keypunch Operators

Data Coder Operators
Terminal Operators
Data Entry Clerk

### Office Machine Operators

Photocopying Machine Operators
Duplicating Machine Operators
Mailing Machine Operators
Addressing Machine Operators
Folding Machine Operators
Inserting Machine Operators
Collator Operators
Coin Machine Operators
Proofing Machine Operators
Billing Machine Operators
Calculating Machine Operators
Bookkeeping Machine Operators

### Secretaries

Legal Secretaries
Medical Secretaries
Technical Secretaries
Administrative Secretaries
School Secretaries
Membership Secretaries

## Reception

### Receptionists

Appointment Clerks
Information Clerks
Classified Ad Clerks

### Telephone and Teletype Operators

Central Office Operators
Directory Assistance Operators

Long Distance Operators
PBX Operators
Communication Center Operators
Telephone Answering Service
 Operators

### *Messengers*

Outside Deliverers
Bank Messengers
Merchandise Deliverers
Copy Messengers
Office Helpers
Route Aides

### *Front Desk Clerks*

Hotel Clerks
Reservation Clerks

# CONSTRUCTION OCCUPATIONS

Occupations requiring specialized skills in working with building materials, to be used on roads, houses, office buildings, and other structures.

### *Painters*

Paperhangers
Shipyard Painters
Maintenance Painters

### *Plasterers & Drywall Installers*

Lathers
Tapers
Sheetrock Applicators
Stucco Masons

Drywall Applicators
Molding Plasterers

### *Cement Masons*

Concrete and Stone Finishers
Concrete Rubbers
Terrazzo Workers

### *Glaziers*

Glass Installers
Stained Glass Glaziers

### *Carpenters*

Maintenance Carpenters
Acoustical Carpenters
Rough Carpenters
Siders
Shipwrights
Form Builders
Joiners
House Repairers
Panel Installers
Roof Assemblers

### *Bricklayers*

Brickmasons
Stonemasons
Tilesetters

### *Plumbers and Pipefitters*

Gas Main Fitters
Pipe Installers
Steamfitters
Furnace Installers
Oil-Burner Servicers and Installers
Steam Service Inspectors
Industrial Pipe Fitters

Gas Meter Installers
Water Meter Installers

## *Floor and Carpet Layers*

Floor Covering Installers
Soft-Tile Setters

## *Roofers*

Roofer Applicators
Gypsum Roofers
Vinyl Coating Roofers
Aluminum-Shingle Roofers
Asphalt, Tar, and Gravel Roofers
Wood-Shingle Roofers

## *Solar Technicians*

Solar-Energy-System Installers
Solar-Energy-System-Installer Helpers

## *Construction Laborers*

Highway Maintenance Workers
Hod Carriers
Pipelayers
Jackhammer Operators
Signalers
Cleaners
Insulation Workers
Asphalt Rakers
Floor Sanding Machine Operators
Concrete-Wall-Grinder Operators
Demolition Specialists
Construction Blasters
Asphalt-Mixing-Machine Tenders

## *Railroad Laborers*

Track Repairers
Track-Surfacing Machine Operators

Track-Moving Machine Operators
Railway Equipment Operators

# ELECTRICITY AND ELECTRONICS OCCUPATIONS

Occupations that require a knowledge of and a skill with electricity and electronics that workers use to construct, install, and maintain electrical/electronic equipment.

## Electricity

### *Linepersons*

Line Installers
Line Maintainers
Line Erectors
Trouble-Shooters
Cable Installers-Repairers
Cable Splicers

### *Electricians*

Electrical Repairers
Electrical Motor Repairers
Powerhouse Electricians
Substation Electricians
Relay Technicians
Voltage Testers
Airport Electricians
Electric-Distribution Checkers
Power-Transformer Repairers
Equipment Installers
Locomotive Electricians

Protective Signal Installers and
Repairers
Neon-Sign Servicers
Street-Light Servicers

## Technical Electronics

### *Broadcast Technicians*

Sound Engineers
Microwave Technicians
Recording Engineers
Audio Operators
Video Operators
Transmitter Operators
Maintenance Technicians
Field Technicians

### *Electronics Technicians*

Electronics Testers
Semiconductor Technicians
Instrumentation Technicians
Laser Technicians
Electrical Equipment Testers

## Manufacturing Electronics

### *Electronics Assemblers*

Electrical-Motor-Control Assemblers
Wire Coilers
Coil Winders
Electronics Utility Workers
Electric-Motor-and-Generator
Assemblers
Transformer Assemblers
Precision Assemblers
Capacitor Assemblers
Electro-Mechanical Assemblers

## ENGINEERING AND DESIGN OCCUPATIONS

Occupations that utilize scientific and design skills to plan and design machinery, buildings, and other structures.

## Engineering

### *Engineers*

Agricultural Engineers
Petroleum Engineers
Nuclear Engineers
Mining Engineers
Ceramic Engineers
Chemical Engineers
Biomedical Engineers
Metallurgical Engineers
Industrial Engineers
Electro-Optical Engineers
Computer Engineers
Human Factors Engineers
Aerospace Engineers
Civil Engineers
Structural Engineers
Architectural Engineers
Sanitary Engineers
Irrigation Engineers
Transportation Engineers
Electrical Engineers
Electrical Test Engineers
Electrical Design Engineers
Electrical Research Engineers
Electronics Engineers
Mechanical Engineers
Automotive Engineers

Tool Designers
Plant Engineers
Marine Engineers

### Engineering Technicians

Electrical and Electronic Engineering
   Technologists and Technicians
Civil Engineering Technicians
Industrial Engineering Technolo-
   gists and Technicians
Mechanical Engineering Technolo-
   gists and Technicians
Chemical Engineering Technicians
Metallurgical Technicians
Agricultural Engineering Technicians
Optomechanical Technicians
Research Mechanics

## Planning

### Urban and Regional Planners

Land Use Planners
City Planning Aides
City Planning Engineers
Program Services Planners

### Architects

Landscape Architects
Marine Architects
School Plant Consultants
Architectural Designers

## Surveying and Drafting

### Surveyors

Land Surveyors
Marine Surveyors
Geodetic Surveyors

Geophysical Prospecting Surveyors
Photogrammetrists
Map Editors
Mine Surveyors

### Surveyor Helpers

Surveyor Instrument Assistants
Chief of Party
Sounders
Geodetic Computers

### Drafters

Architectural Drafters
Civil Drafters
Electronic Drafters
Mechanical Drafters
Landscape Drafters
Electrical Drafters
Structural Drafters
Aeronautical Drafters
Cartographers
Detailers
Checkers

### Interior Designers & Decorators

Display Designers
Merchandise Displayers
Decorators
Display Managers

## FOOD PROCESSING OCCUPATIONS

Occupations in which workers
clean, pack, and convert raw food
stuffs into baked goods, packaged

fish and meats, canned fruits and vegetables, and bottled drinks.

## Bakers

Bread Bakers
Cake Decorators
Head Bakers

## Meat Cutters

Meat Butchers
All-Round Butchers
Chicken and Fish Butchers

## Food Processing Workers

Dough Mixers
Grain Mixers
Flour Mixers
Blenders
Batter Mixers
Chopping-Machine Operators
Cutting-Machine Operators
Feed Mixers
Drier Operators
Oven Operators
Grinder Operators
Decorators
Meat Trimmers
Meat-Grading-Machine Operators
Nut-Sorter Operators
Cheesemaker Helpers
Dairy Processing Equipment
   Operators
Sandwich Machine Operators
Picklers
Candymakers
Noodle Press Operators
Winery Workers

## Cannery and Frozen Food Workers

Agricultural Produce Sorters
Seafood Processing Workers

# FOOD SERVICE OCCUPATIONS

Occupations in which workers prepare and serve foods and beverages, as well as clean up afterwards, in various kinds of restaurants.

# Cooking

## Chefs and Dinner Cooks

School Cafeteria Cooks
Pastry Chefs
Sous Chefs
Specialty Cooks
Restaurant Cooks
Institution Cooks

## Fry Cooks

Short Order Cooks
Pizza Bakers
Grill Cooks

# Serving

## Bartenders

Bar Attendants
Taproom Attendants

## *Waiters and Waitresses*

Hosts and Hostesses
Head Waiters/Waitresses
Formal Waiters/Waitresses
Informal Waiters/Waitresses
Dining Car Waiters/Waitresses
Buffet Waiters/Waitresses

## *Counter Attendants*

Fountain Servers
Cafeteria Counter Attendants
Canteen Operators
Hospital Food Service Workers
Coffee Shop Counter Attendants
Lunchroom Counter Attendants

## Other

### *Kitchen Helpers*

Dishwashers
Pantry Goods Makers
Coffee Makers
Salad Makers
Sandwich Makers
Bakers Helpers
Kitchen Food Assemblers
Pastry-Cook Helpers

### *Buspersons*

Dining Room Attendants
Cafeteria Attendants
Bartender Helpers
Counter-Supply Workers

# GRAPHIC ARTS OCCUPATIONS

Occupations requiring a variety of specialized skills that are used to design and print materials such as books, catalogues, posters, newspapers, and displays.

Graphic Artists and Designers
Industrial Designers
Commercial Designers
Illustrators
Technical Illustrators
Package Designers
Fashion Artists
Medical and Scientific Illustrators
Cartoonists
Animators
Art Directors
Layout Artists
Creative Directors

## *Photographers*

Still Photographers
Photojournalists
Commercial Photographers
Aerial Photographers
Scientific Photographers
Biological Photographers
Camera Operators

## *Printing Production Occupations*

Linotype Operators
Phototypesetter Operators
Typesetting Machine Tenders

Make-Up Arrangers
Compositors
Lithographic Photographers
Lithographic Artists
Strippers
Assemblers
Lithographic Plate Makers
Offset Press Operators
Offset-Plate Makers
Web-Press Operators
Printers
Photoengravers
Bookbinders and Bindery Workers

# HEALTH SERVICE OCCUPATIONS

Occupations requiring workers to use a variety of skills to treat the health needs of patients.

## Treatment and Diagnosis

### *Physicians*

General Practitioners
Family Practitioners
Internists
Surgeons
Pediatricians
Gynecologists
Radiologists
Pathologists
Anesthesiologists
Cardiologists
Obstetricians
Allergists-Immunologists
Ophthalmologists

Podiatrists
Psychiatrists

### *Physician Assistants*

Child Health Associates
Orthopedic Physician Assistants
Urologic Physician Assistants
Surgeon Assistants
Emergency Room Physician Assistants

### *Chiropractors*

### *Pharmacists*

Community Pharmacists
Hospital Pharmacists

### *Occupational Therapists*

Industrial Therapists

### *Activity Therapists*

Recreational Therapists
Manual-Arts Therapists
Art Therapists
Music Therapists

### *Physical Therapists*

Corrective Therapists

### *Speech Pathologists and Audiologists*

Speech Therapists
Speech Clinicians

### *Veterinarians*

Veterinary Anatomists
Veterinary Bacteriologists
Veterinary Epidemiologists

Veterinary Parasitologists
Veterinary Pathologists
Veterinary Pharmacologists
Veterinary Physiologists
Veterinary Virologists
Veterinary Livestock Inspectors

### Optometrist

### Dieticians

Clinical Dietitians
Dietitian Consultants
Teaching Dietitians
Community Dietitians
Research Dietitians
Dietetic Technicians
Nutritionists

### Dentists

Orthodontists
Oral Surgeons
Prosthodontists
Oral Pathologists
Public Health Dentists
Pedodontists
Periodontists
Endodonists

### Dental Hygienists

## Nursing

### Registered Nurses

Hospital Nurses
Private Duty Nurses
Office Nurses
Community Health Nurses
School Nurses

Occupational Health Nurses
Nurse Midwives
Nurse Practitioners
Nurse Anesthetists

### Licensed Practical Nurses

Surgical Technicians

### Emergency Medical Technicians

Ambulance Drivers
Ambulance Attendants
First Aid Attendants
Paramedics

## Assisting

### Nurse Aides and Orderlies

Birth Attendants
Geriatric Aides
Home Health Aides
Psychiatric Aides
First Aid Attendants
Occupational Therapy Aides

### Dental Assistant

### Medical Assistants

Blood Bank Assistants
Laboratory Assistants

## INVENTORY CONTROL OCCUPATIONS

Occupations in which workers handle, store, and keep track of goods and materials during production and distribution.

## Freight Handlers

Longshore Workers
Warehouse Workers
Loaders
Loader Helpers
Material Handlers
Airline Ground Crew Members
Cargo Handlers

## Shipping and Receiving Clerks

Shipping Order Clerks
Reconsignment Clerks
Routing Clerks
Floor-Space Allocators
Sorters-Pricers
Distributing Clerks
Route-Delivery Clerks
Incoming-Freight Clerks
Booking Clerks
Container Coordinators
Cargo Agents
Mailers

## Stock Clerks

Inventory Clerks
Parts Clerks
Order Fillers
Self-Service Store Clerks
Supply Clerks
Procurement Clerks
Quality Control Clerks
Yard Clerks
Merchandise Distributors
Stock Control Clerks

Space-and-Storage Clerks
Truckload Checkers
Property Custodians
Parts-Order-and-Stock Clerks
Store Laborers

## Mail Carriers

Rural Mail Carriers

## Postal Clerks

Mail Handlers
Mail-Distribution-Scheme Examiners
Direct Mail Clerks
Registered Mail Clerks
Parcel Post Clerks

## Newspaper Carriers

Newspaper Delivery Drivers

## Packers and Wrappers

Hand Packagers
Machine Packagers
Masking-Machine Operators
Baling-Machine Tenders
Bundle Tiers and Labelers
Carton-Packaging-Machine Operators
Case Packers and Sealers
Agricultural Produce Packers
Craters
Binder-and-Wrapper Packers
Production Packers
Shipping Packers
Grocery Baggers

# LEGAL, EDUCATIONAL, AND SOCIAL SERVICE OCCUPATIONS

Occupations in which workers aid the development of individuals through education, guidance, recreation, corrections, and related services.

## Guidance

### Counselors

Mental Health Counselors
Rehabilitation Counselors
Career Counselors
Employment Counselors
School Counselors
Guidance Counselors
Resident Counselors

### Social Workers

Child Welfare Caseworkers
Family Caseworkers
Social Group Workers
Medical Social Workers
Psychiatric Social Workers
School Social Workers
Delinquency Prevention Social
   Workers
Community Organization Workers
Human Relations Counselors

### Parole and Probation Officers

### Social Service Aides

Case Aides
Group Work Program Aides
Employment and Claims Aides
Eligibility Workers
Insurance Clerks
Eligibility-and-Occupancy
   Interviewers
Application Workers

### Lawyers

Criminal Lawyers
Corporation Lawyers
Labor Lawyers
Public Defenders
District Attorneys
Judges
Hearings Officers

### Legal Assistants

Paralegal Assistants
Contract Clerks
Legal Investigators

### Psychologists

Clinical Psychologists
School Psychologists
Industrial Psychologists
Experimental Psychologists
Developmental Psychologists
Personality Psychologists
Social Psychologists
Physiological Psychologists
Counseling Psychologists

### Clergy

Clergy Members

Directors of Religious Education
Directors of Religious Activities

# Education

## *Child Care Workers*

Child Care Attendants
Children's Institution Attendants
Nursery School Attendants
Playroom Attendants

## *University and College Teachers*

Atmospheric, Earth, Marine, and
  Space Sciences Teachers
Biological Sciences Teachers
Chemistry Teachers
Physics Teachers
Natural Sciences Teachers
Psychology Teachers
Economics Teachers
History Teachers
Political Science Teachers
Sociology Teachers
Social Sciences Teachers
Engineering Teachers
Mathematical Sciences Teachers
Computer Science Teachers
Medical Science Teachers
Health Specialties Teachers
Business, Commerce, and Marketing
  Teachers
Agriculture Teachers
Art, Drama, and Music Teachers
Physical Education Teachers
Education Teachers
English Teachers
Foreign Language Teachers

Law Teachers
Social Work Teachers
Theology Teachers
Trade and Industrial Teachers
Home Economics Teachers

## *Elementary & Secondary Teachers*

Vocational Education Teachers
Industrial Arts Teachers
Performing Arts Teachers
Preschool Teachers
Special Education Teachers

## *Educational Program Specialists*

Educational Consultants
Instructional Materials Directors
Public Health Educators
Agricultural Extension Agents
Home Economists

# Recreation

## *Coaches*

Sports Instructors
Head Coaches
Professional Athletes Coaches

## *Recreation Directors & Supervisors*

Recreation Superintendents
Recreation Establishment Managers
Recreation Center Directors
Camp Directors
Winter Sports Managers

### Recreation Leaders

Tour Guides
Activity Specialists
Camp Counselors
Hunting and Fishing Guides
Travel Guides

### Recreation Attendants

Recreation Facility Attendants
Bowling Floor Desk Clerks
Locker-Room Attendants
Ski Tow Operators
Skate Shop Attendants
Golf Range Attendants
Ride Operators
Ride Attendants

## Library

### Librarians

School Library Media Specialists
Acquisitions Librarians
Classifiers
Catalogers
Bibliographers
Special Collections Librarians
Children's Librarians
School Librarians
Audiovisual Librarians

## LITERARY OCCUPATIONS

### Freelance Writers

Playwrights
Poets

Prose, Fiction, and Nonfiction Writers
Screen Writers
Humorists
Correspondents

### Writers and Editors

Reporters
Technical Writers
Copywriters
Newspaper Editors
Publications Editors
Story Editors
Book Editors
News Editors
Assignment Editors
Copy Editors
Aquisitions Editors
Production Editors

## MATHEMATICS AND COMPUTING OCCUPATIONS

Occupations that require the use of numerical and data processing skills to solve problems, analyze results, and make decisions in fields such as science, industry, and management.

### Mathematicians and Statisticians

Actuaries
Mathematical Statisticians
Financial Analysts
Applied Statisticians
Statistical Analysts

## *Systems Analysts*

Computer Analysts
Business Systems Analysts
Operations Research Analysts
Electronic Data Processing Systems
  Analysts
Scientific and Technical Systems
  Analysts

## *Computer Programmers*

Business Programmers
Scientific Programmers
Systems Programmers
Numerical Control Tool Programmers
Process Control Programmers
Information System Programmers

## *Computer Operators*

Computer Operations Supervisors
Small-Scale Computer Operators
Computer Peripheral Equipment
  Operators
Tabulating Machine Operators

# MECHANICAL OCCUPATIONS

Occupations in which workers
use specialized mechanical skills
to repair and maintain both large
and small equipment.

## Mobile Equipment

### *Automobile Mechanics*

Tune-Up Mechanics
Brake Repairers

Transmission Mechanics
Front End Mechanics
Automotive Electricians
Radiator Mechanics
Carburetor Mechanics
Air Conditioning Mechanics
Clutch Rebuilders
Muffler Installers

## *Truck and Heavy Equipment Mechanics*

Diesel Mechanics
Industrial Truck Mechanics
Construction Equipment Mechanics
Logging Equipment Mechanics
Air Compressor Mechanics

## *Farm Equipment Mechanics*

Farm Machinery Set Up Mechanics
Sprinkler-Irrigation Equipment
  Mechanics
Tractor Mechanics
Dairy Equipment Repairers

## *Aircraft Mechanics*

Airframe and Power Plant Mechanics
Rocket Engine Mechanics
Flight Test Shop Mechanics
Aircraft Body Repairers
Aircraft Rigging and Controls
  Mechanics
Fuel Systems Maintenance Workers
Aircraft Accessories Mechanics
Field and Service Mechanics
Airplane Electricians

## Small Engine Repairers

Small Engine Mechanics
Outboard Motor Mechanics
Motorboat Mechanics
Power Saw Mechanics
Motorcycle Repairers
Gas Engine Repairers

## Service Station Attendants

Gas and Oil Servicers
Tire Repairers
Automobile Service Station
  Attendants
Automobile Self-Service Station
  Attendants
Industrial Garage Servicers
Vehicle Cleaners
Lubrication Servicers

## Oilers

Stripping-Shovel Oilers
Loading-Shovel Oilers
Greasers
Agricultural Equipment Greasers

# Heavy Machinery

## Mechanics

Industrial Machinery Repairers
Maintenance Mechanics
Machinery Erectors
Machine Assemblers
Treatment Plant Mechanics
Forge Shop Machine Repairers
Gas Welding Equipment Mechanics
Hydraulic Press Servicers
Press Maintainers

Pneumatic Tool Repairers
Hydroelectric Machinery Mechanics
Powerhouse Mechanics
Factory Maintenance Repairers
Automated Equipment Engineers-
  Technicians
Forming-Machine Upkeep Mechanics

## Heating and Cooling System Mechanics

Hot Air Furnance Installers and
  Repairers
Refrigeration Mechanics
Oil Burner Servicers and Installers
Environmental Control System In-
  stallers and Servicers
Evaporative Cooler Installers
Air Conditioning Installers and
  Servicers

# Small Machinery

## Office Machine Repairers

Typewriter Repairers
Cash Register Servicers
Calculating-Machine Servicers
Duplicating-Machine Servicers
Mail Processing Equipment
  Mechanics
Dictating and Transcribing-Machine
  Servicers
Statistical-Machine Servicers

## Computer Maintenance Technicians

Electronics Mechanics
Field Engineers

Electronics Sales and Services
Technicians

### Telephone Installers and Repairers

Station Installers and Repairers
Telephone Maintenance Mechanics
Central Office Repairers
Central Office Installers
Frame Wirers
Trouble Locators
Instrument Repairers
Transmission Testers
Private Branch Exchange Repairers
Private Branch Exchange Installers

### Radio and TV Service Technicians

Radio Repairers
Tape Recorder Repairers
Audio/Video Repairers
Cable Television Installers
Radio Mechanics
Television Installers
Public Address Servicers

### Appliance Repairers

Electrical Appliance Servicers
Electrical Appliance Repairers
Vacuum Cleaner Repairers
Electric Tool Repairers
Household Appliance Installers
Household Appliance Repairers

## Instruments

### Jewelers

Watch Repairers
Engravers
Stone Setters
Silversmiths
Chain Makers
Locket Makers
Ring Makers
Bracelet and Broach Makers
Gem Cutters
Gemologists

### Precision Instrument Repairers

Calibrators
Instrument Mechanics
Electrical Instrument Repairers
Camera Repairers
Photographic Equipment Technicians
Electric Meter Repairers

Scale Mechanics
Locksmiths and Safe Repairers

## METAL WORKING OCCUPATIONS

Occupations in which workers use specialized tools and machines to shape metal gears, cylinders, heating ducts, auto bodies, etc. and then assemble the parts into finished or semifinished products.

## Refining and Casting

### *Metal Refining Occupations*

Pot Tenders
Tappers
Carbon Setters
Heaters
Furnance Operators
Ore and Metals Mixers
Metal Scrap Drier Tenders

### *Metalworking Patternmakers*

Template Makers
Set-Up Mechanics
Model Makers
Mock-Up Builders
Wood Patternmakers
Plaster Patternmakers
Pattern Molders

### *Molders*

Coremakers
Machine Molders
Mold Dressers
Casters
Mold Makers
Die-Casting Machine Operators
Molding and Casting Machine
  Setup Operators
Molding and Coremaking Machine
  Setters
Metal Mold Makers-Repairers

### *Foundry Workers*

Machine Sand Mixers
Furnance Operators
Tumbler Operators

Casters
Metal Pourers
Grinders-Chippers
Heat Treaters
Steel Pourers
Electroplating Laborers
Metal Tappers

## Machining

### *Tool and Die Makers*

Stamping Die Makers
Trim Die Makers
Die Sinkers
Bench Tool Makers
Die Finishers
Die Polishers
Plastic Tool Makers

### *Machinists*

Automotive Machinists
Maintenance Machinists
Instrument Makers
Experimental Machinists
Machine Try-Out Setters

### *Saw Filers and Tool Sharpeners*

Bit Sharpeners
Tool Grinders
Knife Grinders
Cylinder Grinders

### *Machine Tool Operators*

Automatic Grinder Operators
Milling and Planing Machine Setup
  Operators
Punching and Shearing Machine
  Setup Operators

Rolling Machine Setup Operators

Press and Brake Machine Setup Operators

Drilling and Boring Machine Setup Operators

Grinding, Abrading, Buffing, and Polishing Machine Setup Operators

Lapping and Honing Machine Setup Operators

Numerical Control Machine Setup Operators

Lathe and Turning Machine Setup Operators

Lathe and Turning Machine Operators and Tenders

Milling and Planing Machine Operators and Tenders

Punching and Shearing Machine Operators and Tenders

Rolling Machine Operators and Tenders

Press and Brake Machine Operators and Tenders

Drilling and Boring Machine Operators and Tenders

Grinding, Abrading, Buffing, and Polishing Machine Operators and Tenders

Crushing, Grinding and Polishing Machine Operators and Tenders

Slicing and Cutting Machine Operators and Tenders

Drill-Press Operators

Production-Machine Tenders

Punch-Press Operators

# Metal Joining and Fabricating

## *Ironworkers*

Structural Ironworkers
Reinforcing Metal Workers
Ornamental Ironworkers
Metal Fabricators

## *Boilermakers*

Boilermaker Fitters
Boilerhouse Mechanics

## *Sheet Metal Workers*

Sheet Metal Production Workers
Sheet Metal Lay-Out Workers
Coppersmiths
Tinsmiths
Special Items Fabricators
Sheet Metal Model Makers
Sheet Metal Installers

## *Shipfitters and Riggers*

## *Body and Fender Repairers*

Automotive Painters
Truck Body Builders
Automobile-Body Customizers
Frame Repairers
Automobile-Bumper Straighteners
Shop Estimators
Squeak, Rattle, and Leak Repairers

## *Blacksmith and Forge Shop Workers*

Forge Press Operators
Drop Hammer Operators

Die Setters
Forging-Roll Operators
Steel-Shot-Header Operators

## Welders

Arc Welders
Combination Welders
Gas Welders
Lead Burners
Arc Cutters
Production Line Welders
Production Line Solderers
Torch Solderers
Furnance Brazers
Welding-Machine Tenders
Welding Machine Setup Operators
Soldering and Brazing Machine
   Setup Operators

# MINING OCCUPATIONS

Occupations in which workers remove ore, coal, crude oil, and natural gas from the earth.

## Coal and Mineral Mining Occupations

Mining Machine Operators
Conveyor Attendants
Coal and Ore Processors
Channeling-machine Operators
Shale Planer Operators
Cutter Operators
Crusher Setters
Rock-dust Sprayers
Mining Kiln Attendants
Mining Pellet Load-out Persons

Mining Lab Samplers
Machine Drillers
Quarry Workers
Drilling Machine Operators

## Rotary Drillers

Rotary Derrick Operators
Rotary-rig Engine Operators

## Petroleum Helpers

Roustabouts
Rotary Driller Helpers
Pipe-lines Laborers
Oil Well Service Operator Helpers

# OTHER PRODUCTION OCCUPATIONS

Occupations that require specialized skills to be used in a variety of industries to produce goods and services.

## Petroleum Processing Occupations

Petroleum Refinery Laborers
Compounders
Refinery Operators
Blenders
Crude-Oil Treaters

## Rubber and Chemical Processing Occupations

Glue Mixers
Rubber-Mill Tenders
Extruder Operators

Chemical Mixers
Pumpers
Chemical Operators
Mixers-Blenders

## *Rubber and Plastics Fabricators*

Tire Builders
Plastics Bench Mechanics
Rubber-Goods Cutters-Finishers
Compression-Molding Machine
  Operators
Belt-Press Operators

## *Production Painters and Finishers*

Spray Painters
Brush Painters
Furniture Finishers
Coating-Machine Operators
Sanding-Machine Operators
Waxing-Machine Operators
Varnishing-Machine Operators
Stain Applicators
Dippers and Bakers
Lacquerers
Decorators
Latexers
Shellackers
Touch-Up Painters

## *Photofinishers*

Developers
Print Washers
Photographic Spotters
Automatic Print Developers
Black-and-White Printer Operators

All-Round Darkroom Technicians
Color-Laboratory Technicians
Projection Printers
Photograph Retouchers
Print Controllers
Color-Printer Operators
Cutters
Automatic Mounters
Photo Checkers and Assemblers
Paste-Up Camera-Copy Operators

## *Stationary Engineers*

Refrigerating Engineers
Boiler Operators
Substation Operators
Auxiliary Equipment Operators
Gas-Engine Operators
Hydroelectric-Station Operators
Power-Reactor Operators
Turbine Operators

## *Nuclear Power Technicians*

Decontaminators
Power-Reactor Operators
Hot-Cell Technicians
Scanners
Accelerator Operators
Radiation Monitors

## *Water and Sewage Plant Operators*

Wastewater-Treatment-Plant
  Attendants
Sewage-Disposal Workers
Waterworks Pump-Station Operators
Wastewater-Treatment-Plant
  Operators

Water-Treatment-Plant Operators
Waste-Treatment Operators
Watershed Tenders

### Production Assemblers

Bench Assemblers
Floor Assemblers
Line Appliance Assemblers
Automobile Assemblers
Aircraft Assemblers
Steam-and-Gas Turbine Assemblers
Internal-Combustion Engine
  Assemblers
Hand Riveters

### Handcrafters

Woodworker
Potters
Jewelry Makers
Leatherworkers
Hand Weavers
Candle Makers
Clothes Makers
Metalworkers
Calligraphers

## PERSONAL CARE OCCUPATIONS

Occupations in which workers help people with their personal appearance and hygiene, and help meet their short-term personal needs.

### Hair Stylists

Barbers

Cosmetologists
Hairdressers
Manicurists

### Funeral Directors and Embalmers

Embalmer Apprentices
Cremators

## PROTECTIVE SERVICE OCCUPATIONS

Occupations in which workers are responsible for guarding all types of property, and for the safety of people, as established by public law.

### Law Enforcement Officers

Customs Officers
Fish and Game Wardens
Police Officers
Deputy Sheriffs
Detectives
Investigators
Parking Enforcement Officers
State Highway Patrol Officers
Correctional Officers
Jailers
Bailiffs

### Fire Fighters

Fire Marshals
Fire Inspectors
Forest-Fire Fighters

Fire Lookouts
Fire Rangers
Fire Captains
Fire Prevention Bureau Captains
Battalion Chiefs
Smoke Jumpers
Crash, Fire, and Rescue Fire Fighters
Fire-Extinguisher-Sprinkler Inspectors

### Military Enlisted Personnel

Tank Crew Members
Artillery Crew Members
Infantry Members
Air Crew Members

### Security Guards

Merchant Patrollers
Armored-Car Guards and Drivers
Store Detectives
Bodyguards
Gate Tenders

### Health and Safety Inspectors

Food and Drug Inspectors
Industrial Hygienists
Occupational Safety and Health
  Inspectors
Consumer Safety Inspectors
Environmental Health Inspectors
Building Inspectors
License Inspectors
Industrial Waste Inspectors
Sanitarians
Health Care Facilities Inspectors

# SALES OCCUPATIONS

Occupations in which workers help household and industrial consumers purchase goods and receive supplies. Some only accept payment and package merchandise, while others help customers locate and select products; still others try to persuade customers to buy certain products.

### Sales Representatives

Chemical Sales Representatives
Agricultural Products Sales
  Representatives
Building Equipment and Supplies
  Sales Representatives
Office Machine Sales Representatives
Industrial Machinery Sales
  Representatives
Hardware Supplies Sales
  Representatives
Motor Vehicles and Supplies Sales
  Representatives
Pulp, Paper, and Paper Products
  Sales Representatives
Garments and Textile Products
  Sales Representatives
Manufacturers' Representatives
Sales Engineers
Aircraft Technical Sales Workers
Agricultural Equipment and Supplies Technical Sales Workers
Electronic Equipment Technical
  Sales Workers
Industrial Machinery, Equipment,
  and Supplies Technical Sales
  Workers

Medical and Dental Equipment and
Supplies Technical Sales Workers
Chemical and Chemical Products
Technical Sales Workers
Sporting Goods Sales Representatives
Food Products Sales Representatives

### Securities Salespeople

Securities Sales Agents
Securities Traders
Broker's Floor Representatives

### Insurance Salespeople

Insurance Sales Agents
Placers

### Real Estate Salespeople

Real Estate Sales Agents
Sales Superintendents
Residence Leasing Agents
Building Consultants

### Automobile Salespeople

Automobile Leasing Sales
Representatives
Automobile Accessories Salespersons
Trailer and Mobile Home
Salespersons

### Business Services Salespeople

Business Services Sales Agents
Advertising Sales Representatives
Radio and Television Time Sales
Representatives
Sales-Promotions Representatives
Signs and Displays Sales
Representatives

Printing Sales Representatives
Telephone Services Sales
Representatives
Financial Services Sales Agents
Public Utilities Sales Repre-
sentatives

### Route Salespeople

Sales Route Drivers
Lunch-Truck Drivers
Coin Machine Servicers and Re-
pairers

### Salespersons

Clothing Salespersons
Electronics Products Salespersons
Computer Salespersons
Farm Equipment Salespersons
General Merchandise Salespersons
Household Appliances Salespersons
Auto Parts Counter Workers
Musical Instrument Salespersons
Boat and Marine Equipment and
Supplies Salespersons
Sporting Goods Salespersons
Book Salespersons
Home Furnishings Salespersons
Shoe Salespersons
Hardware Salespersons
Cosmetics Salespersons
Jewelry Salespersons

### Sales Clerks

Coupon Redemption Clerks
Layaway Clerks
Sales Attendants
Counter Clerks

# SCIENCE AND LABORATORY OCCUPATIONS

Occupations which require workers to have a scientific understanding and technical laboratory skills to do research and perform tests for quality control or for diagnosis.

## Science

### Life Scientists

Biochemists
Biophysicists
Biologists
Botanists
Ecologists
Geneticists
Zoologists
Microbiologists
Physiologists
Aquatic Biologists
Plant Pathologists
Anatomists
Pharmacologists

### Physical Scientists

Chemists
Physicists
Astronomers
Environmental Analysts
Materials Scientists

### Earth Scientists

Geologists
Geophysicists
Meteorologists
Oceanographers
Hydrologists
Seismologists
Stratigraphers
Mineralogists
Paleontologists
Petrologists

### Agricultural Scientists

Agronomists
Horticulturists
Soil Scientists
Soil Conservationists
Seed Analysts
Animal Scientists
Viticulturists
Food Technologists
Entomologists
Plant Breeders
Dairy Scientists
Dairy Technologists
Fiber Technologists
Poultry Scientists

## Health

### Medical Laboratory Workers

Medical Laboratory Technicians
Medical Technologists
Medical Laboratory Assistants
Phlebotomists
Blood Bank Technicians
Cytotechnologists
Tissue Technologists
Microbiology Technologists

## *Health Technicians*

Electroencephalograph Technicians
Electrocardiograph Technicians
Audiometrists
Dialysis Technicians
Prosthetists-Orthotists
Orthotics Assistants
Prosthetics Assistants

## *Dental Laboratory Technicians*

Orthodontic Technicians
Dental Ceramists
Denture Contour Wire Specialists
Denture Model Makers

## *Opticians*

Dispensing Opticians
Precision Lens Grinder
Lens Mounters
Hand Lens Polishers

## *Radiologic Technologists*

Radiation Therapy Technologists
Ultrasound Technologists
Nuclear Medicine Technologists
Diagnostic Medical Sonographers
Computerized Tomographers

## *Respiratory Therapists*

## Inspecting

### *Quality Control Inspectors*

Agricultural Commodities Inspectors
Quality Control Technicians
Quality Assurance Inspectors

Mechanical Inspectors
Automobile Testers
Automotive Exhaust Emissions
  Technicians
Pollution Control Technicians
Air Analysts
Engine Testers
Assembly Inspectors
Electrical Inspectors
Internal-Combustion Engine
  Inspectors
Motor and Chassis Inspectors
Fabrication Inspectors
Weld Inspectors

## *Laboratory Testers*

Food Technologists
Metallurgical Laboratory Assistants
Pulp and Paper Testers

## SOCIAL RESEARCH AND PLANNING OCCUPATIONS

Occupations in which workers identify and analyze social problems and events and write about them or plan ways to correct them.

## *Social Scientists*

Political Scientists
Geographers
Historians
Biographers
Genealogists

Market Research Analysts
Sociologists
Criminologists
Industrial Sociologists
Penologists
Urban Sociologists
Economists
Anthropologists
Ethnologists
Archeologists
Artifacts Conservators

## *Social Program Planners*

Economic Development Coordinators
Employment Research and
   Planning Directors
Council on Aging Directors
Social Welfare Research Workers

# TEXTILE AND APPAREL OCCUPATIONS

Occupations in which people make, mend, and clean garments and other goods made of fabric and leather.

## Textile Manufacturing

### *Textile Machine Operators*

Fabric Cutters
Knitting-Machine Operators
Folding-Machine Operators
Drying-Machine Tenders
Blending-Machine Operators

Yarn-Polishing-Machine Operators
Machine Trimmers
Pressing Machine Operators
Winding and Twisting Machine
   Setup Operators
Knitting and Weaving Machine
   Setup Operators
Cutting-Machine Fixers
Weavers

## Apparel Manufacturing

### *Clothes Designers and Patternmakers*

Pattern Graders-Cutters

### *Seamstresses and Tailors*

Alteration Tailors
Dressmakers
Custom Tailors
Garment Fitters
Menders
Shop Tailors
Hand Sewers
Cloth Menders
Custom Sewers

### *Sewing Machine Operators*

Machine Trimmers
Hemmers
Stitchers
Stitch-Bonding-Machine Tenders
Basting-Machine Operators
Drapery Sewers
Carpet Sewers

## Laundry

### *Laundry and Dry Cleaning Workers*

Machine Washers
Hand Launderers
Dry Cleaners
Spotters
Machine Pressers
Flatwork Finishers
Folders
Markers
Dyers

## Other

### *Upholsterers*

Furniture Upholsterers
Automobile Upholsterers
Inside Upholsterers
Slipcover Cutters
Upholstery Trimmers

### *Shoe Repairers*

Cobblers
Luggage Repairers

# TIMBER PRODUCTS OCCUPATIONS

Occupations in which workers cut timber and work in mills to process it into dimension lumber, plywood, paper, furniture, or other wood products.

## Logging

### *Fallers and Buckers*

Tree-Shear Operators
All-Round Loggers
Tree-Cutters
Chainsaw Operators

## Pulp and Paper

### *Pulp and Paper Workers*

Pulpers
Pulp Bleachers
Paper Coaters
Coating Machine Operators
Envelope Machine Operators
Bag Machine Operators
Paper Machine Backtenders
Fourdrinier-Machine Tenders
Recovery Operators
Core Winding Operators

## Furniture

### *Woodworking Machine Operators*

Machine Sanders
Ripsaw Operators
Furniture-Making Machine Operators
Wood Machinists
Furniture Finishers
Turret-Lathe Setup Operators
Veneer-Lathe Operators
Wood-Carving Machine Operators
Wood-Turning Lathe Operators
Router and Planer Machine Setup
   Operators

Sawing Machine Setup Operators
Sanding Machine Setup Operators
Shaping and Joining Machine Setup
  Operators
Boring Machine Operators
Router and Planer Machine Operators and Tenders
Sawing Machine Operators and
  Tenders
Sanding Machine Operators and
  Tenders
Shaping and Joining Machine
  Operators and Tenders
Nailing and Tacking Machine
  Operators and Tenders

### Cabinetmakers

Maintenance Cabinetmakers

# TRANSPORTATION OCCUPATIONS

Occupations involving the moving of passengers and freight from one place to another; skills required in operating transportation equipment and keeping on schedule.

## Routing

### Air Traffic Controllers

Station Air Traffic Control Specialists
Tower Air Traffic Control Specialists
Air Traffic Coordinators

### Railroad Conductors

Passenger Car Conductors
Road Freight Conductors

Yard Conductors
Pullman Conductors

### Dispatchers

Radio Dispatchers
Maintenance Service Dispatchers
Motor Vehicle Dispatchers
Taxicab Starters
Interstate Bus Dispatchers
Work Dispatchers
Maintenance Schedulers
Security Guard Dispatchers
Traffic Dispatchers
Tugboat Dispatchers
Police, Fire, and Ambulance
  Dispatchers

## Operating

### Bus and Taxi Drivers

Day Haul or Farm Charter Bus Drivers
School Bus Drivers
Chauffeurs

### Local Truck Drivers

Delivery Truck Drivers
Garbage Collectors
Light Truck Drivers
Heavy Truck Drivers
Food-Service Drivers
Tow-Truck Operators
Logging Truck Drivers

### Long Haul Truck Drivers

Tractor-Trailer Truck Drivers
Van Drivers

## Heavy Equipment Operators

Operating Engineers
Crane Operators
Derrick Operators
Dredge Operators
Bulldozer Operators
Tractor Operators
Construction Equipment Operators
Asphalt-Paving Machine Operators
Concrete-Paving Machine Operators
Road-Oiling Truck Drivers
Earth-Boring Machine Operators
Pile-Driver Operators
Dump-Truck Drivers
Power Shovel Operators
Drag-Line Operators
Tractor-Crane Operators

## Fork Lift Operators

Straddle-Truck Operators
Kiln-Transfer Operators
Machine Stackers
Industrial Truck Operators
Front-End Loader Operators
Hot-Car Operators
Carrier Drivers

# Other

## Railroad Engineers

Locomotive Firers
Yard Engineers
Locomotive Operator Helpers
Motor Operators
Rail-Tractor Operators
Trackmobile Operators

## Railroad Brake Operators

Road Freight Brake Couplers
Yard Couplers
Passenger Train Brakers
Switch Tenders
Brake Holders

## Deckhands

Quartermasters
Deck Cadets
Boat Loaders
Boatswains

## Ship Officers and Engineers

Tugboat Captains
Barge Captains
Dredge Captains
Derrick-Boat Captains
Ferryboat Captains
Riverboat Masters
Ship Masters
Ship Mates
Ship Pilots
Dredge Mates
Tugboat Mates

## Pilots and Flight Engineers

Commerical Airline Pilots
Helicopter Pilots
Test Pilots
Chief Pilots
Navigators
Flying Instructors

## Flight Attendants

# Appendix 2: Education Index

## DATA

### Business

Accounting
Banking and Finance
Business Management and
    Administration
Health Care Administration
Hotel and Motel Management
Insurance
Marketing and Sales
Medical Records Administration
Real Estate
Secretarial Studies and Office
    Administration

### Computer and Information Sciences

Computer and Information Sciences
Data Processing

### Law

Law

### Library and Archival Sciences

Library Science

### Mathematics

Mathematics

## Physical and Life Sciences

Astronomy
Atmospheric Science
Chemistry
General Physical Science
Geology
Life Sciences
Oceanography
Physics
Science Technologies

### Public Affairs and Protective Services

Criminal Justice
Fire Control
Public Administration
Recreation
Social Service

## THINGS

### Agriculture and Natural Resources

Agricultural Business and
    Management
Agricultural Production and
    Services
Animal Science
Fisheries and Wildlife Sciences
Food Science and Technology

Forest Technology and Products
Forestry and Natural Resources
Horticulture and Landscaping
Marine Technology
Soil and Plant Sciences

## Consumer and Personal Services

Animal Grooming and Training
Custodial Services
Floral Design
Funeral Service
Hair Design
Personal Services
Upholstering and Leatherworking

## Engineering

Engineering
Engineering Technologies

## Equipment and Construction

Auto Body Repair
Aviation Maintenance
Aviation Management
Construction Trades
Drafting
Electricity and Electronics Repair
Flight Training
Gas and Diesel Mechanics
Heating and Cooling Mechanics
Industrial Mechanics
Instrument Repair
Metalworking
Precision Production Work
Small Engine Repair
Vehicle and Equipment Operation

Woodworking

# PEOPLE

## Business

Accounting
Banking and Finance
Business Management and
     Administration
Health Care Administration
Hotel and Motel Management
Insurance
Marketing and Sales
Medical Records Administration
Real Estate
Secretarial Studies and Office
     Administration

## Consumer and Personal Services

Animal Grooming and Training
Custodial Services
Floral Design
Funeral Service
Hair Design
Personal Services
Upholstering and Leatherworking

## Education

Counseling
Early Childhood and Elementary
     Education
Education Administration
Health and Physical Education
Secondary Education
Special Education

## Health

Allied Dental Services
Allied Veterinary Services
Chiropractic
Dentistry
Emergency Medical Care
Medical Assisting
Medical Laboratory Technologies
Medicine
Naturopathic Medicine
Nursing
Optical Services
Optometry
Other Health Technologies
Pharmacy
Public Health
Radiologic Technology
Rehabilitation Services
Respiratory Therapy
Speech Pathology and Audiology
Veterinary Medicine

## Home Economics

Child Development and Child Care
Clothing and Textiles
Dietetics
Food Service
Home Economics

## Law

Law

## Psychology

Psychology

## Public Affairs and Protective Services

Criminal Justice
Fire Control
Public Administration
Recreation
Social Service

## Social Sciences

Anthropology
Area and Ethnic Studies
Economics
General Social Science
Geography
History
Political Science
Sociology

## Theology, Religion, and Philosophy

Philosophy
Religion
Theology

## IDEAS

## Architecture and Environmental Design

Architecture and Environmental
  Design

## Communications

Communication Technologies
Journalism and Communications

## Computer and Information Sciences

Computer and Information Science
Data Processing

## Fine Arts

Art
Dance
Dramatic Arts
Modeling
Music
Photographic Arts
Printing and Graphics

## Letters

English and Literature
Foreign Languages
Liberal Studies
Speech

## Mathematics

Mathematics

## Physical and Life Sciences

Astronomy
Atmospheric Science
Chemistry
General Physical Science
Geology
Life Sciences
Oceanography
Physics
Science Technologies

## Social Sciences

Anthropology

Area and Ethnic Studies
Economics
General Social Science
Geography
History
Political Science
Sociology

## Theology, Religion, and Philosophy

Philosophy
Religion
Theology

# Appendix 3: Leisure Activities

There follows six lists of leisure activities that correspond with your interests as measured by Exercise 11.

These lists suggest activities that might be of interest to you. It does not imply that you will have the necessary skills, only the motivation.

## Practical

Repairing or mending things
Bike or horse riding
Walking/hiking
Camping
Playing football, baseball, hockey, basketball
Making things like model aircraft, dresses, etc., using patterns or instruction kits
Cooking
Gardening
Do-it-yourself
Mountain climbing
Ice-skating
Roller-skating
Aerobic dancing
Skiing
Skin diving/scuba diving
Bicycling alone for exercise
Working out in a gym
Jogging alone
Swimming
Archery
Training animals

Hang gliding, skydiving
Carpentry
Candle-making
Winemaking
Sewing

## Investigative

Developing and processing photos
Reading books and magazines on scientific or technical subjects
Observing, collecting, identifying such things as birds, animals, plants, fossils, shells, rocks etc.
Visiting museums, scientific or technical displays
Watching and listening to documentaries or "in-depth" reports on TV and radio
Playing chess, bridge, scrabble, mastermind, or other games of skill
Computer programming
Genealogy
Self-development
Meditation
Attending lectures

## Social

Visiting and working with the handi-
capped, old people, etc.
Taking part in scouts, youth groups,
etc.
Planning and giving parties
Attending sports events, pop con-
certs, films etc., with a group of
friends
Helping to raise funds for a charity
Working with young children in
play groups, Sunday schools,
scouts, etc.
Activities with the family
Massage
Spending social time with friends, at
clubs, dinner parties, restaurants
Joining clubs or activities primarily
for the social functions e.g.,
church, choral group, Political
party, drama club
Sailing with others
Traveling with friends or in a group
Playing games where winning is
not important

## Artistic

Playing a musical instrument or
singing
Writing short stories or poetry
Sketching, drawing or painting
Taking part in plays or musicals
Craft work, e.g. pottery, weaving,
knitting, jewelry making, macrame
Visiting art galleries, exhibitions,
plays or concerts

Arranging flowers
Yoga
Photography
Gem polishing
Interior decorating
Restoring antiques
Sculpting

## Enterprising

Playing monopoly, backgammon,
poker or other "games of chance"
Doing small jobs, such as gardening
or car repair work for a fee
Taking part in debates or making
speeches
Following politics in the newspa-
per or on radio or TV
Being on a committee
Earning money by selling things
Games where winning is important
Winemaking to save money
Entering craft work in competitions

## Organizational/
## Administrative

Using typewriters, calculators, com-
puters for record keeping
Keeping detailed accounts or a
careful diary
Cleaning
Keeping times and recording re-
sults at sporting events
Collecting and cataloging coins,
stamps, photo albums, scrapbooks
Calligraphy

# Appendix 4: Job Search Tips

Whether you are a newcomer to the business world, or a worker looking for a change, the following guidelines will be helpful to you in your job search.

## Step 1. Build a Support Network

Family, friends, and trusted associates can provide you with valuable insights and support in brainstorming, suggesting job leads, and networking. More importantly, they can provide moral support and encouragement along the way.

The importance of networking in your chosen field cannot be understated. Extend your contacts by joining professional organizations, volunteering in your field, attending seminars and cultivating social contacts. The avenues that open up to you through individual contacts often generate more solid job leads than merely sending out your résumé does.

## Step 2. Research the Job Market

Identify what companies are located in the areas you have selected that also have the type of employment you have determined best suits your career and life goals. Find out as much as you can about each particular company so that you know what type of organization you will be dealing with. Focus *only* on those companies that can offer you positions that you know you want and are capable of handling. Many times there are job openings available that are not advertised through newspaper classified ads. Uncover these through your network of contacts or the human resource departments of your selected firms.

For information on civil service job openings, contact your local state employment agency or Civil Service Commission. They are required to post all job openings and give examinations throughout the year for job openings in a wide variety of professional, technical, and clerical occupations.

## Step 3. Prepare Your Résumé

There are many good reference books that offer specific recommendations for preparing an effective résumé. Your résumé should highlight your specific skills and accomplishments and should be clearly written and logically laid out.

Essential information on what to include in your résumé is:

- Personal Information—Name, address, and telephone number
- Job Objective—Not what kind of job you want, but what *you* can do for your prospective employer
- Educational Background—Name of school(s), degree(s) obtained, major courses of study, dates of graduation. If you are long out of school, it may be irrelevant to list school achievements and extra-curricular activities.
- Work Experience—Job titles and brief description of actual duties, emphasizing the skills employed to effectively accomplish your job. Remember, these skills are transferable to the new position that you are seeking, even if it is in a completely new field. Be sure to include people skills as well as technical skills you have developed.
- References—These should be listed as "Furnished upon request."

When you have drafted your résumé, pass it around to your contacts to see what kind of feedback it gets before finalizing it.

## Step 4. The Interview

Always prepare thoroughly for your interview. Research the industry and the company. Find out as much as you can about the individual doing the interviewing and the specific job opening for which you are applying. This will aid you in presenting the skills and qualifications you possess that would best meet the needs of the prospective position.

- Grooming—Your personal appearance will give the first impression to your prospective employer. Be sure to be neat, clean, and appropriately dressed for the position for which you are applying.
- Communication Skills—The skills you developed through this program are transferable to your interview process as well. Be sure to listen attentively to questions you are asked, respond clearly and concisely, and don't be afraid to ask questions in return. Your communication skills are essential to projecting a confident and enthusiastic image.

- Salary Negotiations—Most counselors recommend that the employer be the first to bring up this subject. If a range is given, express an interest in the top of that range. Your research should have uncovered the prevailing salary range for the type of position you are seeking, so be realistic and flexible in your expectations.
- Follow-Up—No matter what the outcome of your interview, be sure to follow up with a short note thanking the interviewer for his or her time and stating that you will contact them on a specific date. This not only substantiates your courteousness and professional attitude, but allows you to call the employer again to see whether a decision regarding the position has been made. If you are not selected for this position, you can then ask to be kept in mind for future openings.

## Step 5. Stay Flexible

> When we initiate change, we initiate a period of chaos and disorganization. That is the way we bring about something new, the way we create. Remember: before you make an omelette, you have to break eggs.
>
> Pamela Rafferty

Don't be afraid to break a few eggs. Refer back to the exercises you completed in this book to help you reassess yourself and reprioritize your goals as you go through your job search process.

# Resources

# Books

## Career Management

Gilbreath, Robert D. *Save Yourself: Six Pathways to Achievement in the Age of Change.* New York: McGraw-Hill, 1991.

> This book will show you how to take charge of your work life amidst shakeouts, restructurings, and reorganizations.

Hopson, Barrie, and Mike Scally. *Assertiveness: A Positive Process.* San Diego, California: Pfeiffer & Company, 1993.

Hopson, Barrie, and Mike Scally. *Communication: Skills to Inspire Confidence.* San Diego, California: Pfeiffer & Company, 1993.

Hopson, Barrie, and Mike Scally. *Time Management: Conquering the Clock.* San Diego, California: Pfeiffer & Company, 1993.

Hopson, Barrie, and Mike Scally. *Transitions: Positive Change in Your Life & Work.* San Diego, California: Pfeiffer & Company, 1993.

> Four books in an easy to use, open-learning format. Suitable for both individual and group use. These books have been designed to follow the Code of Practice on Quality Open Learning (MSC 1987).

Kannich, Ronald L., Ph.D., and Caryl Rae Kannich, Ph.D. *The Complete Guide to International Jobs and Careers.* 2nd ed. Manassas Park, Virginia: Impact Publications, 1992.

> This book explains the what, where, and how of working in today's highly competitive international job market. It also includes how to start an international business.

Levering, Robert. *A Great Place to Work.* New York: Random House, 1988.

> This book tells you how to spot good places to work, and avoid bad ones. It explains what makes a place good to work at and how to transform a company into a good one, even if you aren't the owner or manager.

Mackay, Harvey. *Sharkproof: Get the Job You Want, Keep the Job You Love...in Today's Frenzied Job Market.* New York: Harper-Collins, 1993.

Otterbourg, Robert K. *It's Never Too Late: 150 Men and Women Who Changed Their Careers.* New York: Barron's Education Series, 1993.

> This book provides information on why people choose to do it and how to do it yourself.

## Job Hunting

Allen, Jeff. *Jeff Allen's Best: Get the Interview.* New York: John Wiley and Sons, Inc., 1990.

Allen, Jeff. *Jeff Allen's Best: The Resume.* New York: John Wiley and Sons, Inc., 1990.

Allen, Jeff. *Jeff Allen's Best: Win the Job.* New York: John Wiley and Sons, Inc., 1990.

Beatty, Richard H. *The New Complete Job Search.* New York: John Wiley and Sons, Inc., 1992.

> Everything from what job you would be good at to how to get it.

Bird, Caroline. *Second Careers: New Ways to Work After 50.* New York: Little, Brown and Co., 1992.

> This book is based on a study by the AARP's *Modern Maturity* and contains information on why people often choose their second career based on considerations other then money. It is useful for people of any age who are considering switching careers.

Bob Adams, Inc. *JobBank Series.*

> Over twenty books on how to find employment in specific cities and states.

Cohen, William A. *Student's Guide to Finding a Superior Job.* San Diego, California: Pfeiffer & Company, 1993.

Kannich, Ronald L., Ph.D. and Caryl Rae Kannich, Ph.D. *The Best Jobs for the 1990's and Into the 21st Century.* Manassas Park, Virginia: Impact Publications, 1991.

> This book describes how changes in the economy, market, and technology will change the job market and how to get into a career that is about to take off.

Montag, William E. *Best Resumes for $75,000+ Executive Jobs.* New York: John Wiley and Sons, Inc., 1992.

> This provides help in writing resumes and cover letters for high-end jobs. It has a section on tough career transitions (including making a transition when you are over fifty) and fifty real life sample resumes.

Morton, Tom. *The Survivors Guide to Unemployment.* Colorado Springs, Colorado: Pinon Press, 1992.

> This includes everything from preparing for impending unemployment to dealing with your emotions and rebuilding your self-esteem to what to tell your family and friends.

Smith, Michael Holley. *The Resume Writer's Handbook.* 2nd ed. New York: HarperCollins, 1987.

Surry Books, Inc. *How to Get a Job Series.*

> More than ten books on specific U.S. cities, Europe, and the Pacific Rim.

Reference books and directories are a valuable source of information in job searches. They are usually available in the main branches of your public library, but if you have access to a university or college library you will also find many specialist reference books not readily available in the local library. You can also contact your local unemployment office, which publishes a variety of free literature.

## Self-employment

Burstiner, Irving. *Start and Run Your Own Profitable Service Business.* Englewood Cliffs, New Jersey: Prentice Hall, 1993.

> This book covers practical concerns like financing, hiring and training, price setting, advertising, insurance coverage, and taxes and includes sample charts and forms.

Frost, Ted S. *The Second Coming of the Wooly Mammoth: An Entrepreneur's Bible.* Berkeley, California: Ten Speed Press, 1991.

> This book contains the nitty-gritty details that every small business owner wishes they had known when starting out.

## Alternative Work Patterns

Alvarez, Mark. *The Home Office Book: How to Set Up and Use an Efficient Personal Workspace in the Computer Age.* Woodbury, Connecticut: Goodwood Press, 1990.

> This contains advice on the practical aspects of setting up a home workspace and how to deal with working alone plus a brand name buyer's guide.

Arden, Lynie. *The Work at Home Sourcebook: Over One Thousand Job Opportunities Plus Home Business Opportunities and Other Options.* 4th ed. Boulder, Colorado: Live Oak Publications, 1992.

> This book details opportunities for telecommuting and home businesses and includes a list of companies and positions available.

Blyton, Paul. *Changes in Working Time: An International Review.* London: Croom Helm, 1985.

Cross, Thomas B. and Marjorie Raizman. *Telecommuting: The Future Technology of Work.* Homewood, Illinois: Dow Jones-Irwin, 1986.

*Internships 1993: The Guide to On-the-Job Training Opportunities for Students and Adults.* 12th ed. Princeton, New Jersey: Peterson's Guides, Inc., 1992.

> This is a directory of positions available.

Swart, John Carroll. *A Flexible Approach to Working Hours.* New York: AMACOM, 1978.

## The Pfeiffer Career Series

Schein, Edgar H. *Career Anchors: Discovering Your Real Values,* Revised ed. San Diego, California: Pfeiffer & Company, 1993.

Smith, Maggie. *Changing Course.* San Diego, California: Pfeiffer & Company, 1993.

# Living in the Information Era

Toffler, Alvin. *The Third Wave.* New York: Morrow, 1980.

> Crucial for an understanding of how the Information Era is fundamentally different from the Industrial Era. Very stimulating, with a global perspective.

Naisbitt, John. *Megatrends: Ten New Directions Transforming Our Lives.* New York: Warner Books, 1984.

The trends for the Information Era identified by a fascinating technique of trend analysis through local newspapers.

Naisbitt, John and Patricia Aburdene. *Megatrends 2000: Ten New Directions for the 1990s.* New York: Morrow, 1990.

Drucker, Peter F. *The New Realities: In Government and Politics, in Economics and Business, in Society and Worldview.* New York: Harper and Row, 1990.

A changing analysis of the information-based organization, the input of knowledge workers on organizations and the economy, and much more.

## Self-development

Deporter, Bobbi, and Mike Hernacki. *Quantum Learning: Unleashing the Genius in You.* New York: Dell, 1992.

This book has techniques to help you learn more and take quantum leaps to career and academic success.

Sheehy, Gail. *Passages: Predictable Crises of Adult Life.* New York: Bantam Books, 1977.

Best seller which charts the progress of adults through all the key life stages. Fascinating case studies enable you to play "spot yourself."

Sheehy, Gail. *Pathfinders.* New York: Morrow, 1981.

An investigation of how satisfied with their lives American men and women are at different periods of the life cycle. It also gives great encouragement to people to take risks in their lives as that seems to correlate highly with reported satisfaction.

## Women

Faludi, Susan. *Backlash: The Undeclared War Against American Women.* New York: Crown Publishing Group, 1991.

Koltnow, Emily, and Lynne S. Dumas. *Congratulations! You've Been Fired: Sound Advice for Women Who've Been Terminated, Pinkslipped, Downsized or Otherwise Unemployed.* New York: Fawcett Book Group, 1990.

This book tells women how to turn being fired into a prime opportunity to make more of themselves and their careers.

Morrison, Ann M., et al. *Breaking the Glass Ceiling: Can Women Reach the Top of America's Largest Corporations?* Updated ed. Reading, Massachusetts: Addison-Wesley Publishing Company, 1992.

Naisbitt, John and Patricia Aburdene. *Megatrends for Women.* New York: Villard Books, 1992.

Sheehy, Gail. *The Silent Passage.* New York: Random House, 1992.

White, Jane. *A Few Good Women: Breaking the Barriers to Top Management.* New York: Prentice Hall, 1992.

> This book describes how to handle sex discrimination and destroys common myths about steps women should take to get ahead by using the real stories of twelve successful women.

## Directories

Dun & Bradstreet's Million Dollar Directory.

Dun & Bradstreet's Reference Book of Corporate Managements.

Moody's Industrial Manual.

Standard and Poor's Corporation Records.

Standard and Poor's Industrial Index.

Standard and Poor's Industry Surveys.

Standard and Poor's Listed Stock Reports.

Standard and Poor's Register of Corporations, Directors and Executives.

## Educational and Training Information

Libraries have college catalogs and guide books and are often drop-off sites for community college and adult education literature. Some libraries also have self-help audio and video tapes available.

## Voluntary Work

### Points of Light

Nonprofit organization devoted to addressing serious social problems by increasing the number of people who serve their communities as volunteers. Gives referrals to local volunteer network that can help you work in your area of interest.

(800-879-5400)

## Health

Benson, Herbert, M.D., and Eileen M. Stuart, R.N., M.S. *The Wellness Book: The Comprehensive Guide to Maintaining Health and Treating Stress-Related Illness.* New York: Carol Publishing Group, 1991.

> This book includes information on exercise, nutrition, stress management, and the mind-body connection of health.

Bortz, Walter M. II, M.D. *We Live Too Short and Die Too Long: How to Achieve and Enjoy Your Natural 100-Year-Plus Life Span.* New York: Bantam, 1992.

> This book presents strategies to add decades of satisfying, active time to your life. It has a program of eight simple physical and psychological directives to get you off to a better, longer life.

Leatz, Christine A., and Mark W. Stolar. *Career Success/Personal Stress: How to Stay Healthy in a High-Stress Environment.* New York: McGraw-Hill, 1992.

> This explains how to transform yourself into a stress-resilient person, even in a pressure-cooker environment.

Shealy, C. Norman, and Caroline M. Myss. *The Creation of Health: The Emotional, Psychological, and Spiritual Responses that Promote Health and Healing.* Walpole, New Hampshire: Stillpoint, 1988.

## Retirement

**AARP (American Association of Retired People)**
601 East Street, N.W.
Washington, DC 20049
(800-453-6609)

> Promotes the interests and rights of older Americans. Offers members referrals to services and advertisers in their publication *Modern Maturity,* offers discounts and other fringe benefits.

Baron's Keys to Retirement Planning Series including *Keys to Understanding Social Security Benefits.*

## For People with Disabilities

Witt, Melanie Astaire. *Job Strategies for People with Disabilities: Enable Yourself for Today's Job Market.* Princeton, New Jersey: Peterson's Guides, 1992.

> This book has information about the Americans with Disabilities Act and making the job fit you. It also contains an extensive resource section.

# About the Authors

# Dr. Barrie Hopson

Barrie is chairman of The Lifeskills Group, which is the leading developer and producer of flexible learning systems for organizations in the United Kingdom.

Previously he was chief executive and then chairman of Hay-Lifeskills, part of the worldwide Hay Group. He was director of the Vocational Guidance Research Unit at Leeds University in Yorkshire and then founded the Counseling and Career Development Unit at Leeds University and was its first director until 1984. He was a visiting professor to the Universities of Oregon, Washington, and Michigan and to JFK University in California.

He has worked widely as a consultant to business and educational organizations in the United Kingdom, Europe, the United States, Canada, and Hong Kong. He was responsible for setting up the first career counseling service in British industry in 1970 (at Imperial Chemical Industry) and has since helped a number of organizations around the world to set up career counseling and career management systems. He is a fellow of the British Psychological Society and of the British Institute of Management and is a professional associate of the National Training Laboratories for Applied Behavioral Science in Washington, DC.

He has written twenty-six books and numerous articles on personal and career development, career guidance, marriage, lifeskills teaching, quality service, transition and change management, and generic training skills.

Barrie's current consultancy activity is largely spent setting up and designing major employee and management development initiatives in companies such as BP, British Airways, BBC, Digital Equipment Company, ICI, Motorola, and Data General.

# Mike Scally

Mike was formerly deputy director of the Counseling and Career Development Training Unit at Leeds University in England. It was there that he and Barrie Hopson developed the "Teaching Lifeskills" approach that had a significant impact on the British education system and eventually instigated projects linking health with increasing self-esteem and empowerment. The increased influence of this approach to promoting self-management eventually took Mike and Barrie into management development in industry and commerce and led them to set up their own company.

Mike has worked as both trainer and consultant, at all levels, from board to front line, in many major organizations. He has led major training and development programs for international airlines and multinational chemical companies, and for companies in the following industries: financial services, leisure and hospitality, retail, brewing, and international trading.

He has also written some fifteen books, and he has lectured at many international management conferences on the themes of career management, creating quality service cultures, and building customer-driven businesses.

Mike also acts as consultant to a range of development agencies that initiate self-help programs in the Third World.

# Index

# G

Gender, expectations based on, 21
Goals
  alternative, 203
  appropriateness of, 20
  changes in, 10
  conflicting or changing, 216-217
Groups, working with, 25-26
Growth occupations, 56

# H

"Having" needs, 57
Heading Cards, 45
Help, asking for, 194-195
Herzberg, Frederick, 58
Hierarchy of Needs, 101-102
Hobbies, 43. *See also* Leisure
Home employment, trend toward, 61
Horizontal career pattern, 111
How Do Others See Me? exercise,
  122-123
How Satisfied Am I? summary
  sheet, 138
Human development, 96-97
Human resources, making use of,
  164
"Hygiene" factors, 58, 59

# I

Idea skills, 65
Imagination. *See also* Creativity
  importance of, 10
  role in exploring possibilities, 13-14
  using, 143-145
Important others, getting feedback
  from, 121-122
Income
  analyzing, 156-159

as an area for change, 17
  relationship to job, 42
Inflation rate, 119
Information-gathering skills, 13
Insights
  keeping a record of, 25
  writing action notes for, 216
Intellectual development in
  adulthood, 98-99
Interests
  analyzing, 72-85
  information gathering about, 12
  types of, 67-69
Interests check, 123

# J

Job complaints, converting into
  objectives, 146-149
Job content skills, 61-63
Job Families, 67
Job-related needs, 160
Jobs. *See also* Careers;
  Employment; Work
  alternative, 48-49
  analyzing, 46-49
  as an area for change, 17
  fantasies about, 143-145
  networking to obtain, 164
  variety in, 160
Job search, tips for, 267-269
Johari Window, 121-122

# K

"Keep a record" files, 24
Key life events, analyzing, 35-36
Know Yourself skills, 11, 12, 213

# L

Learn From Experience skills, 11

Editor:
**JoAnn Padgett**

Assistant Editor:
**Heidi Erika Callinan**

Production Editor:
**Katharine Pechtimaldjian**

Interior Designer:
**Paul Bond**

Cover:
**John Odam Design Associates**

| OF SOME IMPORTANCE | NOT IMPORTANT |
|---|---|

| QUITE IMPORTANT | VERY IMPORTANT |
|---|---|

| IMPORTANT | **PLACE OF WORK** It is important to work in the right part of the country. |
|---|---|

| **PEACE** You prefer to have few pressures or uncomfortable demands. | **VARIETY** You enjoy having lots of different things to do. |
|---|---|

| **COMPETITION** You enjoy competing against other people or groups. | **INDEPENDENCE** You like being able to work in the way you want, without others telling you what to do. |
|---|---|

HAVING

BEING

## TIME FREEDOM

You prefer to choose your own times for doing things versus having rigid working hours.

## FRIENDSHIP

You like close friendships with people at work.

## FAST PACE

You enjoy working at a fast pace.

## STATUS

You enjoy being in a position that leads other people to respect you

## DECISION MAKING

It is important to make decisions about how things should be done, who should do it, and when it should be done.

## CREATIVITY

Thinking up new ideas and ways of doing things is important.

## RISK

You like to take risks.

## EXCITEMENT

It is important to have a lot of excitement in your work.

## MONEY

Earning a large amount of money is important.

## HELP OTHERS

It is important to help other people, either individually or in groups, as part of your work.

|  |  |
|---|---|
| **DOING** | |
| **DOING** | |
| **BEING** | |
| | **BEING** |
| | **HAVING** |

## WELL-KNOWN ORGANIZATION
You like being part of a well-known organization.

## PROMOTION
You like to work where there is a good chance of promotion.

## CHALLENGE
You enjoy being 'stretched' and given new problems to work on.

## ROUTINE
You like a work routine that is fairly predictable.

## PRESSURE
You like working to deadlines.

## COMMUNITY
You like to live where you can get involved in the community.

## WORK WITH OTHERS
You like to work in a team alongside others.

## PHYSICAL CHALLENGE
You enjoy doing something that is physically demanding.

## WORK ALONE
You like to work on your own.

## ARTISTIC
You enjoy work involving drawing, designing, making music, making models, etc.

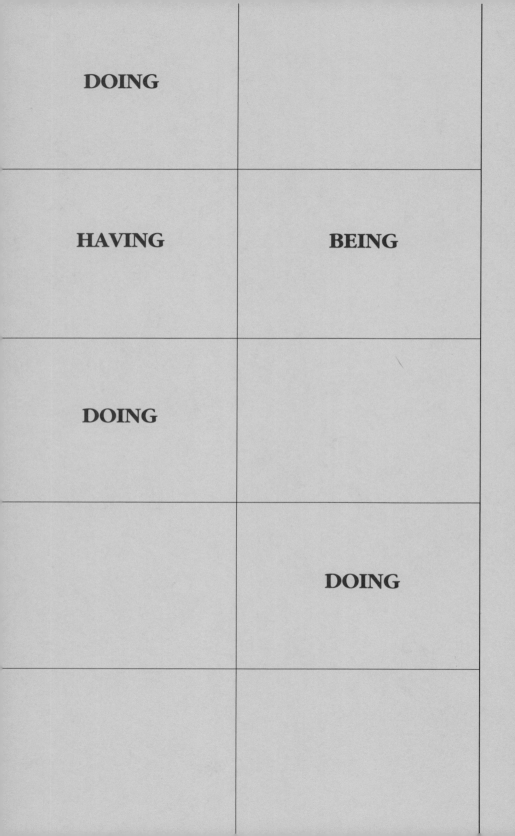

DOING

HAVING

BEING

DOING

DOING

## COMMUNICATION
You enjoy being able to express ideas well in writing or in speech.

## RECOGNITION
You like people to appreciate you for the work you do.

## SECURITY
It is important to know your work will always be there for you.

## CONTACT WITH PEOPLE
You enjoy having a lot of contact with people.

## PRECISE WORK
You like working at things that involve great care and concentration.

## HELP SOCIETY
You like to think that your work is producing something worthwhile for society.

## SUPERVISION
You enjoy being responsible for work done by others.

## PERSUADING PEOPLE
You enjoy persuading people to buy something or change their minds about something.

## LEARNING
It is important for you to learn new things.

## BEING EXPERT
You like being known as someone with special knowledge or skills.

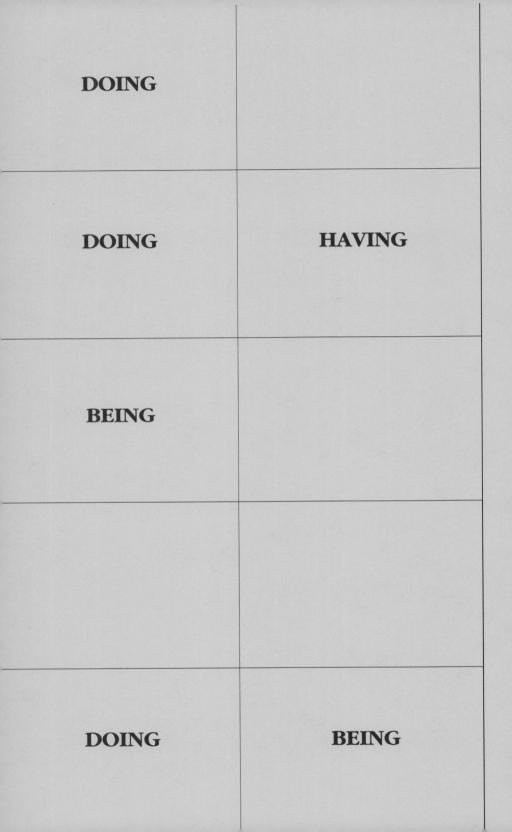

DOING

DOING                    HAVING

BEING

DOING                    BEING

| VERY COMPETENT | COMPETENT | ADEQUATE FOR TASK |
|---|---|---|
| UNDEVELOPED | P<br>Drawing out people | T<br>Hand-eye coordination |
| T<br>Keeping physically fit | T<br>Using hand tools | T<br>Handling things with precision and speed |
| T<br>Assembling things | T<br>Fixing, repairing things | D<br>Analyzing, dissecting, sorting, and sifting through information or things |
| T<br>Building, constructing | T<br>Muscular coordination | D<br>Problem solving |
| T<br>Finding out how things work | T<br>Physically strong | D<br>Reviewing, evaluating |
| T<br>Driving car, motorcycle | T<br>Quick physical reactions | D<br>Diagnosing, looking for problems |
| T<br>Manual dexterity | T<br>Using machine tools, sewing machine, lathe, power tools, etc. | D<br>Organizing, classifying |

| | | |
|---|---|---|
| D<br>Reading for facts | D<br>Following instructions, diagrams, blueprints, etc. | I<br>Creating, innovating, seeing alternatives |
| D<br>Researching, gathering information | I<br>Working creatively with colors | I<br>Sizing up a situation or person quickly and accurately |
| D<br>Manipulating numbers rapidly in mental arithmetic | I<br>Conveying feelings or thoughts through drawing, painting, etc. | I<br>Having insight, using intuition |
| D<br>Calculating, computing | I<br>Fashioning or shaping things or material | I<br>Reading for ideas |
| D<br>Memorizing numbers | I<br>Working creatively with spaces, shapes, or faces | I<br>Developing others' ideas |
| D<br>Managing money, budgeting | I<br>Composing music | I<br>Conveying feelings or thoughts through body, face, and/or voice |
| D<br>Examining, observing, surveying, an eye for detail and accuracy | I<br>Improvising, adapting | I<br>Writing creatively |
| D<br>Taking an inventory | I<br>Designing things, events, learning situations | P<br>Conveying warmth and caring |

| | | |
|---|---|---|
| P<br>Helping others | P<br>Taking first move in relationships | P<br>Promoting change |
| P<br>Giving credit to others, showing appreciation | P<br>Motivating people | P<br>Leading, directing others |
| P<br>Listening | P<br>Organizing people | P<br>Showing sensitivity to others' feelings |
| P<br>Selling, persuading, negotiating | P<br>Teaching, training | P<br>Performing in a group, on stage, in public, etc. |
| | | |
| | | |
| | | |
| | | |